NOTES TOWARD
A SUPREME FICTION

Prolegomena to the Narrative Sublime

A Theory of Fiction

NOTES TOWARD
A SUPREME FICTION

Prolegomena to the Narrative Sublime

MARK HENDERSON

After the Works of Harold Bloom

indubitable precursor to descendant ephebe

A bench was his catalepsy, Theatre
Of Trope. He sat in the park. The water of
The lake was full of artificial things...

There was a will to change, a necessitous
And present way, a presentation, a kind
Of volatile world, too constant to be denied...

                    It was not a choice
Between, but of. He chose to include the things
That in each other are included, the whole,
The complicate, the amassing harmony...

It is possible, possible, possible. It must
Be possible. It must be that in time
The real will from its crude compoundings come

                         Stevens

A KIND OF INTRODUCTION

These philosophical remarks, prolegomena to a theory of fiction, have been printed as originally conceived and composed, provisionally set out, in relation to the writing of a novel called *Abandoned By The Gods*. Here, they are preserved in the material immediacy of their contingent thought—even when generative misreadings—as a critical placeholder for further investigation. They bear directly upon the formal, historical, and aesthetic aspects of narrative as an embedded practice of the body-mind, one analytically grounded in the constraint of the phenomenal, the actual, the cultural. In their compression and ellipticality of prose, corrective in *clinamen*, however provisional and broad in nature, the reader may find, within the form of the philosophical argument, a literary logic of some interest and instruction, if not pleasure, as in the reading of poetry.

BOOKS

I. IT MUST BE ABSTRACT

II. IT MUST CHANGE

III. IT MUST GIVE PLEASURE

BOOK ONE
IT MUST BE ABSTRACT
FORM

BOOK TWO
IT MUST CHANGE
HISTORY

BOOK THREE
IT MUST GIVE PLEASURE
INTEREST

BOOK ONE

IT MUST BE ABSTRACT

ON THE VISIONARY
ARRANGEMENT OF A WORLD

FIRST ANIMATION and FORM. *And some say that soul is intermingled in the universe, for which reason, perhaps, Thales also thought that all things are full of gods—Aristotle, De Anima (On The Soul).* Souls and gods are come on in us. Come now out about us from us. We have put the word to the world. A long time now souls and gods are come about us from us. We want them in the world beyond the word real in ontic aspect and it is of no matter. The world is dead to us but for a story of the world. Already one must speak of it so to make it live. This is not a practice of our time. It is a practice of all times. Represented times. One has seen and felt some atavistic thing. One has felt some seen thing in material want. Souls and gods are come about us. They are not to be so easily believed. But in us. We cannot have them so easily believed but in want of them to be. We tell of them at storied length. They need not be sacred. We say things held to be sacred. The first secular substance the unseen world of gods. Of ancestral spirits. It is the beginning of an art. There is an old craft of the self. The animation of the world in a critico-mythico narrative. A first form of knowing. The psychic- shamanistic nature of the world put up in words. The nature of phenomena. Pictured. It is epi-phenomenal. Imaged. It is not the world. It is the nature of our want. It is somatic-cum-psychic want put over against the world. It is the beginning of aesthetic order. There is a figured reason come into being for all come about us in us. A metaphysic. Metaphysics a prosody. Morphology. Language meta-form for phenomenal experience. It is the beginning of the necessity of narrative. The transcendence of object into image. The seen into symbol. Day night into duration. All the onto-cosmogonic immanence of the world yet to be known. Epistemology to be. To be known once formed into word. But first ideography. Picture word. Picture first. Before being spoken to form. Picture. It is already an aesthetic. There are aesthetics. The act of the image. The animation of the world under a principle of formal abstraction. Experience preserved in mimetic ideation by hand. Paint on rock. Composition. The emergence of the somatic-psychic under the propensity of want in a world. To narrative. But picture first. All narrative rising from out of the phenomenal. And moving back within one so. Then epiphenomenal. After ideography. Lines and signs become symbol. There is talk of souls. We call out for gods. It is the beginning of some trage-dy. It is already lyrical. Some first abstraction of feeling into form. Ontic abstraction first a human act moving in a mortal logic toward the sublime. Terror and transport phenomenal ground. All told picture seen against phenomenal ground. A first vision and arrangement of feeling thinking materially formed. Symboled so. An empirical prescience. All figure pictured in duration in distance against body-mind. That palpable time-space. Dynamics of the aesthetic. Somatic terror and psychic transport made visionary arrangement by hand across rock by eye. By hand the immanent world rearranged in mimetic shamanism. Representative picture. We have put the world into word. We want. We abstract. We animate. We arrange epiphenomenally in the image of the phenomenal. We see surfaces and call out for gods and souls. In the magnitude of immeasurable things we call out for significance. For selves. It is an old form.

WANTING FIGURED or the MAKING SEEING. *And the tale is not mine but from my mother, how sky and earth were one form; and when they had been separated apart from each other, [they] bring forth all things, and gave them up into the light; trees, birds, beasts, the creatures nourished by the salt sea, and the race of mortals—Euripides, Melanippe the Wise.* The creation of the world is not pictured so. Until it is told. What is seen is seen then so. Creation story. Pictured. The abstraction and arrangement of a world into narrative begun in picture. All persons places things brought forth by eye in word. Lately. Long before a written word a picture. The nature of the world abstracted and arranged under a mortal want into picture. Picture the beginning of supreme language. Ideography of image. Picture first narrative before one told thing spoken to form. Ideographic sense from the seen. Nothing has been spoken to form. All is somatically seen. The psychic transport of simile in epic the emotive force of catharsis in tragedy unwritten unknown to the eye in rock painting in the dark of the cave. Yet there they are fore-figured in the dark of the cave long abstracted and arranged in mythopoetic tones. Unnamed pre-historical trope. First mythopoeia. There supremely visionary in their dark quiet reverberating in an atavism which yet lingers on. Though they have only been lately seen so. In their art resides the mortal want of visionary form. It is the mortal no turned toward a yes. There is purpose in their painting. There is possibility in their painting. Well one must get one's self round the world. The past is remembered. The future projected. All as if upon a screen in the principled animation of the human eye cast upon rock risen from inside a point of view where all is at stake. There in that form the somatic-psychic induction of an aesthetic some millennia before the writing of the first science or the play of high affect. The cosmogony of the world made in a dark vision from a motive want the first presentation of the human read written so in picture. The world captured in visual arrangement necessary aesthetic ontically seen and felt and reseen in principled form abstracted under mortal necessity. It is enough to be born. The necessity of the lived experience the predicament. True art all visionary arrangement an abstraction of such individual necessity however general the form. A craft of the self. Such sublime experience first wanting containing form. The expression before the concept. Seeing-feeling constraining a technique into an art. But no contemporary convention. It is an old phenomenal form. A proliferating craft of the authenticating self. The act of authorial abstraction formed in alchemic transcendence of sense to symbol sensation to symbolization under motive want knowing no stock history no worn word but first experience formed. Phenomenal constraint. Aesthetics the epiphenomenal. The meta-phenomenal considered act of the remembered and the projected figured-as-picture. Metaphysic form. Metamorphic. All supreme art an act of transcendent necessary vision in visionary arrangement. The ontic re-presentation of picture the first true fictive form. Imaged paint painting the induction of the somatics of psychic want into picture. Figure the aesthetic deduction made out of the reality of the body the mortality of the body. Sight and sense only made so in mortal want. Aesthetics an act of abstraction of no reality without somatics made psychic. Transcendence of object to image. There is a supreme narrative. That is the analytic. It is beyond taste. It knows no correctness. A visionary method. A phenomenology of form. All visionary form true and real a picture of somatic-psychic space-time. Narrative of the most human. We are human. Vision unearthed. That deductive ground. Vision unearthed to indelible image in remembrance and projection made material under the logic of a history of somatic wants. That temporal distance of the past to the conditional for picture in duration. It is lyrical. The self having found itself. An excess of psychic sight immanently presented pictured. In the priority of the ontically seen. Experience pictured. The epiphenomenal first formed informed from the phenomenal. That induction. Never otherwise. That secondary order for an extant real in ideographic duration. Until remade in its real. In reading-seeing. In narrative. Then all the world pictured under the propensity of want. Presentation of palpable sight. That painting a singular act of self more than ever the representation of a world. In excess of the world. Expressive solipsistic self. Abstraction cast affectively into visionary form not representation per se. All mimesis all sheer mimesis necessary and problematic for vital expressive narrative. Ideographic animation. A critical problem of perception. Atavistic aesthetics. Of object to image. Of distance-duration. No category of classical mimesis. No mirror-like effects per se. Expressivity seen. All effect some atavistic somatics made present in an eye to word. An affected eye. Narrative epiphenomenal transcendence of object to image. Then story. That experiential necessity of image. Palpable. Dynamically formed psychological space felt more than thought to be seen. That livid matter of the mind. Dramatic real. The story of a lived dire picture. The scope of something sublime. Yet no theory of picture. Picture pictured. Not yet one word in the light. A grand ocular animation cast across rock in dark. Already a supreme invention of solipsistic self. A soul before the concept acting as a god when there are none.

THE OBJECT as if THE REAL. *And now, I said, let me show in a figure how far our nature is enlightened or unenlightened: —Behold! Human beings living in an underground den, which has a mouth open towards the light... [And] they see only their shadows, or the shadows of one another, which the fire throws on the opposite wall of the cave?...[A]nd then conceive someone saying to [them], that what he saw before [inside] was an illusion, but that now, when he is approaching [outside] nearer to being and his eye is turned towards more real existence, he has a clearer vision, —what will be his reply? And you may further imagine that his instructor is pointing to the objects as they pass and requiring him to name them, —will he not be perplexed? Will he not fancy that the [inside] shadows which he formerly saw are truer than the [outside] objects which are now shown to him? Far truer. And if he is compelled to look straight at the [outside] light, will he not have a pain in his eyes which will make him turn away to take refuge in the [inside] objects of vision which he can see, and which he will conceive to be in reality clearer than the [outside] things which are now being shown to him? True he said—, Socrates to Glaucon, Plato, Republic, VII.* Visionary arrangement has long been antithetical to mimesis. Mimesis holds a claim to the true. The real. We do want the correspondence of the world as a true model for the real. That is true. Strict mimesis holds an object as a claim to the real the true. This is an unanimated fact. Phenomenal immanence. Necessary but not sufficient. For narrative. The strict representation of the actual. As if the world without word. All what is ontologically seen is held to be true. Real. Well we want the real real. We yet see by two eyes. The mind's within the ontic. The mimetic object is split from within out without in. Vision becomes visionary. Vision must become visionary. In narrative the actual symbolic. This is the crux of an art. Remember vision must become visionary. Know this one thing if nothing else. What is seen so must be reseen. All else follows from the translation of thing to thingness. It is then great books are to be written. Then the truly realistic. The real of realism. Then the romancing of the real at last a supreme narrative in mimesis as a transcendence of vision. The visionary arrangement of the ocular the true real as imaged picture figured of the subject. The true real of narrative a figure come in backward round from the world out the eye of the body-mind. All visionary visions inducted of necessity no less the true or real of the mimetic object however of a diegetic figure. All is of a figure. All is of a shown figure but told subject. In narrative. Ontological sight the most minor figure to be held as a flat fact. For nothing may be said of it. May be made of it. It is the blank stare of a blind eye. Not a mind's eye. Then narrative the furniture of inert rooms. The conventional of convention too familiarly seen. Sheerly mirrored. The end of an imagination. Until reseen. Diegetically seen. Now something must be said of it mortally seen. All what is ontically seen. Or nothing new is made. There remains the old immanent ontic. It is necessary. But we form in our feeling for mortal sight. If at all. Look. What is seen is somatic. What is at stake is psychic. But what is symboled is transcendent. Metamorphic. Dialectic in diegetics. In France as it is now known in Chauvet cave of the Ardeche as it is now named the animation of narrative resides in the psychic abstraction of the somatic. Of affective feeling formed in transcendent effect. Pictured effect. In ocular transcendence of the ontic to the symbolic. Sensation to symbol. It is a world more significantly real to its maker as an object made image than the object of the ontic world which it represents. It is some first transcendence of the all too ontic object into a supremely expressive first subject. A still life gallery reverberating in somatic propensity toward supreme power of psychic transport. Aestheticized sight. Already it is a major aesthetic. The world is creatively alive. Mimetic shamanism. Made diegetic. Mimesis turned trope here in transcendence of expressive somatic lividness. To narrative. A transformation of matter made of mind. Psychic play of the mind's eye pictured. No sheer ontological materialism for the eye. Expression cannot be exhausted or reduced by the abstracting eye. Necessary expression cannot be exhausted or reduced to the sheerly seen. All expressive sight of no known rote convention. There is not one convention known. The world is unknowingly alive. The world is alive as never before. Or again. No paraphrase. There is open-ended parameter. This is not a contradiction in form. It is form. The constraint is the phenomenal. The mortally seen. Represented. In it never the convention of taste. No a priori idea-view. Representation presentation. What is felt to be seen. All is at stake. What is so formed reseen. All sight reformed in what is necessarily phenomenally recurrently risen to transcendent image. Regeneration recurrence. This is the epiphenomenality of supreme narrative. In it diegetic continuity. However elliptical. The symboled mind's self-told time. There is a hand and a color and an eye. A cagey artist. The phenomenality of the eye follows the propensity of feeling. A first phenomenology of form. Of a narrative self-projection. The first great fiction pictured upon rock in dark. A self-projection made visible. A dramatic logic. A story. At last a mode of keeping the self. Preserving the self. A methodology of self-preservation in each such diegetic projection. In craft a craftsman. In considered craft a craftsman preserved. Almost a character. The painter-narrator as character. Before a notion of antiquity a primal artist extant in onto-Paleolithic time livid in Aurignacian narrative indelible in red ochred charcoaled image animated picture in strata of stone. Sublimely interned. The deep time of affective picture. All confounding time kept superimposed in supremely aestheticized picture. We see it.

We know it. We know it in our time. We have never known it. We have never seen it so. Yet we see it so. Now we see it. In our propensity we know its art. Luckily the lineage. No matter time. We look in self-recognition. The atavism of the aesthetic. That is the rich view. There is a long view of aesthetics. All how a primal scene of craft works. All how one eclipses convention for form in the mortal. In supreme form representation refigured in sublimely livid picture turned. Mortally troped. The great solipsistic aside. A first soliloquy. That crafty turn from the actual in form. In art first intimations of the immortal. Picture projected in possibility. Toward preservation. Toward narrative capability. Toward aestheticized self out of sheer actuality. Nothing is lost. In the end there is the phenomenal. That is the end. But that supreme art not ideally epiphenomenally ever lost to it. All is to be gained in it. No ends in the epiphenomenal. No overcoming extant actual in the vital form of it. The actual overcome in the aesthetic. In the act of reverberating form. No void to come. All is beginning. Present in the vivid persisting epiphenomenal real. The future lasts forever. Unreached.

VISION as ABSTRACTION against CONVENTION. *For by the original composition of the universe sky and earth had one form, their natures being mingled; after this their bodies parted from each other, and the world took on the whole arrangement that we see in it—Diodorus I, 7, I.* From the long view of aesthetics as that which is rich in lived life and deeply held in some inexplicable true feeling for the world visionary form is the beginning of the battle against convention. Even when at first unrecognizable as such. It is against false feeling. It is an expressive presentation however abstract of a claim for the true. The true is often unrecognizable in form. In its palpable constraint. Not the representative convention of a claim for the true made without the constrained expressive presentation. It is the presentation of the human out of some stylized feeling if not original composition of the sky and earth. The arrangement of a picture of first feeling is already of form but not convention. It is abstraction but not reductively abstract. It is enactment. Expressively real. It is mimetic but not representative in claim. Again it expressively presents so to claim. From phenomenal induction of its forms. To the vivid limits of its perceptual constraint. That is the formal morality of an arrangement. The good of form. It enacts if not an original composition of the earth and sky then a composition of a never repeated never repeatable human time held in and to the limits of a perceptual constraint. Deep real. However recurrent in repetition of person place or thing in duration. Its recurrence is phenomenal. Atavistic in its narrative epiphenomenality. Ancestrality of aesthetic. For the human is held when time is held. Diegetic duration. Time is held on in a mortal picture. There is a moral form. Holding the human in its deep real. It is normative. Not ideological. Not of taste. It allows the appearance of the critically human. Such holding is a moral form. No matter abstract. The human appears most alive in it however good. The human appears most true however good. Such holding is a battle. It is all already the battle of a necessary deep vision come against a necessary form-convention. And we must have form. It is necessary as nothing else. No matter that the familiarity of the contemporarily seen can kill a feeling so formed. History wants to dictate to experience. The history of representation wants to dictate to the never repeatable actuality of experience. There is a leisure a comfort a too familiarity an ease of the actual which kills the true feeling of picture. The actual is familiarized. Degrades to formal habit. There are limits to expression. To lives. To time. It is almost the loss of an art. The de-animation of the however unknown real the actual of the lived life the unsettledness of the seen and felt in psychic-somatic time to the degradation of the ordinary as the actual. The actual is never ordinary. It is the ground of transcendence. Then a reduction in vision almost the loss of an art. One of our late weaknesses of sight. A problem of clock time. The subject measured in so many sentences. The object in so many words. The attenuation of image. The human. One must pass over. To what? To what is simply next. Pace. Brevity with little to no wit. Essence. This faked false ordinariness contriving the poverty of scene. Plot passing for story. Action for affection. The ordinary for the actual. The psychic residue of the individual the never repeatable subject materially lost as a quality of the image in a picture devoid of its mortal time and space held in its recurrent spots however elliptical in the discontinuity of an expressive vital art. Lost in convention. There are limits to expression. It is held to be so. Picture become habit. Cinema photography. Snapshot. Sheer mimetic exposure. The deep time undone. Form become fixed convention in material reproduction without vital necessity. And no living organism does that. Is never that unfamiliar with itself. As form. In time. Distance. Duration. And cannot be if to live. To express vitality. Such fake fixed form not an epiphenomenal induction of any necessary organics. Art divided from the phenomenal real. The however real world object itself no longer a dialectical project in narrative to be. A phenomenal reality subsumed under the epiphenomenal qualitative never repeatable view of the subject in mortal time amplified to image. Symbol. The psychic subject mind informed formed in the somatic object body in natural order as of day or season or year. That is how supreme narrative lives. The epiphenomenal infused to it formal limits with the ontic residue of the phenomenal. And round back again. And no living organism that loses that lives. Nothing living does that. Loses that and lives. Why not an art? Why not aesthetic vitalism? Being is formed in the constraint of immanent principle. So too supreme art. Not in a cult of ideology. Institutionality. Not in such trite times of passing taste. Passing taste frames out in stock forms truths without apt tropes no wise mortal turns amplified formed from the transcendence of the actual troped toward the aesthetic. The real true. Taste sketches paraphrase for form. The necessity of form fossilized into a dead thing. Speaking preformed not necessary. Not performed of vital necessity. Livid form. We must have vital expressive necessity of livid form. There is no artistic language without it. There is no living language. Narrative alive epiphenomenally. This is not a contradiction in ontological category. A mortal life is rhetorical of necessity. A rhetoric. It is the question of how to say. There is an organic rhetoric in the somatic-psychic. We must find it. We have seen it. It is formal however historical. That is the crux. Already in the first paint on rock it is the argument of how to see so to say. An ancient act of abstraction now become the first problematic of form. Yet it lay before all history of aesthetics. A hidden revelation. Arrangement made of no convention. No taste. Originary in convention before the concept. The extraordinary actual abstracted into first picture. Mortal form. An original composition of the lately human.

ON THE SOMATIC ARGUMENT
AGAINST A WORLD

SOLIPSISM as WRITING or ARGUMENT. *Robert Cohn was once middleweight boxing champion of Princeton. Do not think that I am very much impressed by that as a boxing title, but it meant a lot to Cohn—Hemingway, The Sun Also Rises.* Writing of any style contains a rhetorical attack. Writers attack. It is a form of authenticity. Writers write out of a posture of some troping defense. Narratives move that way too. An angle of attack on the world and on others in it as if all is already somehow against speaking. All is against speaking. One wants to speak. One must take a stance to be heard. We hear Hemingway. The rhetorical movement is always away from relation to argument. Diegesis turned to claim. Defense. Performance. Whether one of a narrator or a writer. One presents an argument in all supreme scenic structure. A strong writing is this express formal movement in prose from a relation to a compression of a particular stance. That is the form of the two Hemingway sentences. The first sentence is expository. It relates. Exposition moves to become presentation. Reportage is subsumed by performance in the second. It is solipsistic such formal movement. It is a dramatic compression. It is a voice. It is a voice that carries the character. Presents to preserve character. It is the drama of the self formed in the sentence as a kind the self presented in a language as a quality. It is more about personality than picture. Yet there is great clarity. It gives up a picture of the self. It enacts personality. It is character picture. It is acutely performative. It is not abjectly descriptive. It is an act of disclosing personality. It is a compression of personality which privileges declarative attack against the propriety of strict mimetic convention for character. Interiority of illustrating character. The shown told. Diegesis framing mimesis. Speakers who are personalities feel the immanence and immediacy of solipsism in the face of history. Writers speaking-craftsmen women transcend the phenomenal world in narration. Yet writing an ontic written out act. Art ever framed in the actual. Writing posited as a worldly stance. First an expression of experience as a form of language. Not sheerly the content of a subject. While necessary cause a subject subsumed here however necessary. Yet the subject infusing the form. The content of the form. Dialectic diegesis. We are two sentences in and the subject is the subject of the self. It is the nature of the attack. It is the quality of the defense. It is the kind of narrative argument. Strong writing the abstraction of somatic feeling cast into the formal figure of an argument for the self. Its genesis that psychic space.

It paints scenes to hold that animated space. From somatics picture. It finds its language stood so. Becomes visionary turning itself into a mortal-moral language. Formal preservation. Stands noble eloquent putting the self against the simply seen. Such language is for the good of the self. Whatever the good of the writer. The self figured-as-spoken against the given world. All attacks are tropes of the self. Stances figures for the self. All for the good of the self. Writers know that. Writers do that. Writers above all make and do that. Writers do that when claiming not to do that. Language become vital in that. Speakers character. Narrative personality. The language lives as its speaker must. It is a true fiction. The vivid picture of vital character spoken into being. We hear who one is in a word. We hear how a character-narrator let's just say a writer in supreme narrative is alive on a page as an argument a metamorphic kind a life-quality performed. World-making. Self-making. Narration as personality is transcendent and psychically lived. From the actual to the art as actual. Books come into being by act. Generative propensity. The atavism of the art is the artist. There is an actual aesthetic enactment of idiosyncracity. A speaker with a stake in a world in a sentence in a book. Somatics makes a style. Authenticity is a heard thing. The self necessarily declared. In a book. Necessity become declaration. Style strong declaration made in the quality of a spoken position a view wherein a self in a world is at stake. The world framed so and in such a way. And why not if so declared and believed in in a book as in a life? However of invention? A psychic stance as a form of language is a quality of livid declaration. Such declaration set out in epiphenomenal ontology. Art as actual. But never without the actual. Phenomenal. We have put the word to the world. The supreme narrative real ever to be an act of the real real. Ever without it while within it. That is the narrative effect of the elemental figure as a kind. Declaration is ontological. The ontological put so and in such a way first a focus of the self. Narrative ontology not the world. The self against the world. The world is in it. An affected act of language for all things. A picture put in particular focus from feeling. That psychic distance run on somatic stance. All objects become subjects in their closeness or farness of picture of attack. We hear an argument for the self in the spoken closeness to persons and things. Distinctions made. Richness in the closeness-farness of pictured-time to from persons places things. How the human is held. Formed. Focused. Who speaks and how. Who looks and how. There is an apt psychic distance to be held in all somatic stance as picture. Temporal distance. It is dialectical. No analytic or supreme idea perceived in narrative but in this seen language so to legitimate a speaker and their world as spoken. In form a real brought into being wherein an analytic an idea may be grounded. In a self at stake. That ground for all proliferating epiphenomenal thought of any necessary form. Who speaks and why? Therein the how. The self affects language as a form. Longinus says style is the shadow of a personality.

Language as a style is an act of the legitimation of a narrative self. To want to speak. To want to speak strongly is an argument for the authenticity of the narrative self. Narrative a taken-up position stood in and held out of felt necessity onto so to expand in a spoken quality of holding a particular kind of world across all scene and action. Form somatic stance pictured in a held onto language. Or one should paint nothing. Write nothing if it is not. For one can see nothing strongly present against one's self. Nothing necessary. Nothing to be held clearly and truly. The self is not implicated. The invention is too narrow. The picture out of kilter. There is nothing to authoritatively declare. Nothing to speak of. Then one should say nothing. For there is nothing of necessity to declare. Immanent interest. For one argues against nothing present. There is nothing present against one's speaking as a substantive act. No ontological declaration. Perhaps there is representation. But no ontological declaration for the narrative self. Perhaps there is the mimesis of the object. Devoid of the subject. The semblance of the world. In a semblance of the world. For then it is all as one may say a conventional representation. No matter its mimetic form. We do not hear how this writing can be other. Cannot be other. It is wanting form. It is a problematic of form. Of distance and declaration. Of the found language for the picture. Of what and how to put the picture when and where. The narrative as a spoken integrity seen so and only so in its organic algorithm. Of being on a page. Of how to abstract the real real.

Not via paraphrase. The very lack of paraphrase. A progressive necessity of stance. Fictive form a motive power spoken. The authentic generation of style-subject in word found out from ontic-object in world. One's subject at hand in the distance between the word as a spoken quality and the ontic object at hand. Image-forming. Mimetic-diegesis. It is dialectical. No narrative limits to the language of such declared transcendence from thing to thingness in the angle of attack. A point of view made prophetic in its want turned to the figure of attack. A point of view is a self at stake. A point of view is a stake in the world. The strong voice is a trope. One must see something strongly present against one's self. One must want to speak of it. One authenticates in degrees of want. All objects are animated in want. Words as though compulsory in want. The aesthetic scope of this somatic act cannot be contained by the individual proposing it as an art of psychic want. Transcendence.

SOLIPSISM or VOICE in ARGUMENT. *That we were formed then say'st thou? and the work of secondary hands, by task transferred from Father to his Son? Strange point and new! Doctrine which we would know whence learnt: who saw when this creation was? Remember'st thou thy making, while the Maker gave thee being? We know no time when we were not as now; know none before us, self-begot, self-raised by our own quick'ning power, when fa-*

*tal course had circled his full orb, the birth mature of this
our native heav'n, ethereal sons. Our puissance is our own,
our own right hand shall teach us highest deeds, by proof
to try who is our equal: then thou shalt behold whether by
supplication we intend address, and to begirt th' Almighty
throne beseeching or besieging—Milton, Paradise Lost V.*
All language put to tell us the true has a necessary posture
of self-power. The particular reality of any narrative however general in its human concerns is brought into its being most forcefully through the stance of a voice believing
wholly in its own power to make the world. A supreme narrative makes its own word and light. All made out of the somatic stance the spoken word and light of a Lucifer feeling
what should be. Somatic narrative a revolution of the self-
begotten self. One is never too late. History cannot matter.
There has never yet been one true story. That actual trumps.
There is much at stake in speaking such a way. There is a
claim for the world and the people in it in speaking such a
way. We hear the dramatic. Life is at stake. It is the narrator-
self against all. All is to be gained or lost. A word here or
there is all the difference. All turns and is held on some few
words. All actuality is compressed. All a way of speaking.
All somatic argument a dramatic compression. Speaking in
such-a-way a dramatic compression. This is the way it is. No
other. No matter history. No matter the history of literature
full of such solipsistic speakers from the Greeks to the Moderns. One must feel. One yet does. All narrative of any con-

sequence to others and itself is run upon a speaker's having taking up some dire stance against the world even if comedic in degree. The somatic is the mortal power of the comedic too. And the analytic as argument too. Narrative generality all analytical argument of some any kind of normative claim come as comment judgment aside monologue soliloquy in narrative language most true and general when most solipsistic in its scenic generation pictoral presentation however large or small the canvass however elliptical or durational the time-place the very shortness of image placed unfolded held in particularity to anchor the claim individually sensually somatically. If shortness richness. The particular life unfolded in narrative picture in the felt-to-be-lived allows the generality of diegetic comment as true. Particular speaking put so against the world in a normative language is most truest and general when most solipsistic and that is not a contradiction. It cannot be otherwise. It is that the normative or the rule of the real declared in scene or told as outright revelation is an induction of the actual as the phenomenal. It is that real. What is felt is the actual and the true. In a supreme narrative there is an essential tension between the intellect and the act. This dialectic tension in narrative is not contradictory. The conventional is eclipsed in the actual of the intellect. Intellection act. The somatic-psychic. Truth appears. There is a singular voice speaking out of what all feel. It makes the general particular. It is long familiar yet new in its never repeatable singular algorithmic poetic. It is a prosody of the recognizable yet the argument has never once been made so. We have not yet ever heard it put so. Distinctive discriminating tenor-tone. No matter we have long felt it so. This singular voice takes up a position for all. In the prosody of its stance it speaks for all. It speaks against material immensity immanence history the framed self the circumscribing world for all. It begins a defense of all in its particular feeling. Feeling for life. To reframe all. For it is then in this individual position having been taken up as a kind of defense of all as a singular voice set out in scene and picture in all that may be lived and felt that all the constraints of the world that all social and historical and cultural cants against the self will appear in some congregated unison and come against one strongly and truly come to all implicated selves put so in a life spoken so of and so lived so to reframe all no matter in a book. Heard so in reframing it is supremely felt and lived. And now against that very individuality of speaking constrained so by the congregation of the world come about it in pictured story it is then that the general appears in some truth out of the particularly felt. There is a story. It is the generality of the individual predicament phenomenally pictured in a time and place and humanly held and in that duration in its distance it is not a clock time. The epiphenomenal actual of the predicament. All a somatic-psychic time. The ranging acuteness of a sensing consciousness. That wide-ranging perceiving picture all what implicates the text with the true. Generality in narrative appears most truly and strongly against such a taken up particular position of the self held out onto palpably durationally in narrative in solipsistic form. And we see in our reading-seeing in our hearing-experience of narrative as if experiencing a life lived that there is nothing worth going on with in narrative without the argument and defense of the self spoken so strongly across the page as if one's own self necessarily so moved somatically across the world. One is so moved in the actual. It is dramatic. There is ontological drama. It is more than a drama. There is the lived excess on the page brought back to the actual. The somatic space of supreme narrative become the moral implication of the reader. The morally implicated reader authenticating the actuality and interest of the fiction. It is true. There is much to feel. Much to lose. The reader is situated so. There is a mortal distance. One closes upon it. And now when the individual situated so in such a language one that is a primary argument for the self first above all there all the general principles of why this somatic mortal self will not long last in a world appear. There is only so much time. We feel what is gone. Think to what is left. There is dramatic and moral interest in the realization of mortal time. This temporal distance an epiphany. The real of realization. There is no clock time here. However the intimation of shortness measured in it. The somatic heard pictured extended amplified as if sanctified in its one unrepeatable never to be again significance. This felt time of the body-mind is not clock time. It is the aesthetic time of the argument made and taken to generalize the predicament of the individual. Some little regret or hour of the self become the span of a book. A remembrance the argument of a voice. All is felt. The utterance is left. We do not last long. We speak against things. We must speak against things. We cannot long last. That is why we speak so.

ON THE PSYCHIC SHAPE
OF A NARRATIVE WORLD

THE OBJECT of ANIMATION. *When the categories of subject and object, both insoluble in the critique of knowledge, come to appear false—as not purely opposed to each other—this also means that the object's objective side, the part of it which cannot be spiritualized, is called 'object' only from the viewpoint of a subjectively aimed analysis in which the subject's primacy seems beyond question. Viewed from the outside, that which in reflecting upon the mind appears specifically as not mental, as an object, is material. The category of nonidentity still obeys the measure of identity...Neither the subject nor the object are merely 'posited,' in Hegel's manner of speaking. This alone explains fully why the antagonism which philosophy clothed in the words 'subject' and 'object' cannot be interpreted as a primal state of facts—Adorno, Negative Dialectics, 192-94.* Let me tell you there is no positivism no sheer materialism in the objects of the narrative world. Quite unlike history or philosophy or science as they are held to be practiced the facts the ideas the knowledge in a narrative world exist superimposed in time and space first as vital entities resonant with a lived-in view unfolding out informed by while informing the language of a speaker. Collapsed category. Vitality is the somatic stance of the speaker in possession of an argument no matter how god-like or mortal in collapsing the object into an image. Symbolized subject into psychic shape. The psychic solipsism of this posture practice however wide and far-reaching beyond the individual is what animates all single objects casts all within a necessary language of things persons and places circumscribed by a vital consciousness placing itself so round the world and for some argued-reason felt. There are souls and gods come about us in us in the art of animation. For the self-begotten speaker the soul is first psychical. More than sheer consciousness. Beyond mimetic perception. Narrative space is the lived traversing of a psychological space along a country a road a town. That is its kind. How it is done in degree with what things what persons and what places is a question of the quality of the speaker and the argument ever informing that language. And language may make any quality of such a kind. No the real that is true in a fictive form is not ever a presence or state brought into being by the descriptive the factual the act of the catalogue though it may depend upon such minor figures. The animation of a narrative of moral and mortal interest no longer has objects per se as the world but consists of a mental-emotive landscape of resonant subjects posing yet as objects of a world. The symbolic is psychic. The object transcends its surface mass in the mentally palpable claim of the declarative word. The animation of the ontological in the epiphenomenal. Now nothing is dead in such a narrative. The animation of things in such a narrative not ever the real brought into being in an art in the naming of a thing alone as an inert surface transcribed representation of the actual. No transcription in narrative. Transcendence. Transcription ever only some seeming real that is not ever true appearing actual. Some minor god presiding over the soulless. A typist. Weakness worded. Falseness of form that is not ever the presentation of a lived psychic life amongst the objects which congregate about a livid logic in some true relation of never repeatable recognizable familiarity however recurrent in their being kept at hand and in such a close kept way put to that very life lived once and only so once in a necessary and mortal relation to them. In a claim for a symbolic order animated so congregated in circulation superimposed so one must have transcendence not transcription. This long the problematic of representation of supreme narrative art. It is the problematic of enduring narrative space. The mimetic necessary yet not sufficient. A supreme art whether over its own durational time or that of immanent history however drawn in narrative space-time is the presentation of a consciousness caught in its most lived-in corners in its very expressive act of coming to be in a world however it may want to talk on at length of showing all the world first as objects held in hand so to have the real before itself. It is only to reframe the real. That is its mimetic game. However close or far the people places and things of the world are in distance-duration they are held diegetically in against a speaker a speaker who speaks-in-such-a-way of them in their real speaks in a psychic excess across the page animates the actual into the symbolic. Well one must tell one's self a story of the self and the world to get anywhere even in the world for good reason. Or it is all dead convention all ordinary roteness abject ritual nothing significant. All is significant. Nothing is ordinary. In a supreme art the actual as a true real comes always to be from within out and when it turns and it does so toward the world it turns then mostly to itself in its necessary solipsism in its most mimetic places and persons and things. The picture it makes in closing the psychic distance between objects and its speaking of objects its subjects symbols significances all that the animation of a style. A personality. The reflection of a quality of mind. The shadow of a personality. A pictured presentation of subject in all object. That is its look its language its look. There are no false objects. All mirrors lit from within in such word of the seen. All objects spiritualized.

The OBJECT of TELLING a SHOWING. *That was the beginning of a series of most interesting and most unusual lectures which my father, inspired by the charm of that small and innocent audience, delivered during the subsequent weeks of that early winter. It is worth noting how, in contact with that strange man, all things reverted, as it were, to the roots of their existence, rebuilt their outward appearance anew from their metaphysical core, returned to the primary idea... "The Demiurge," said my father, "has had no monopoly of creation, for creation is the privilege of all spirits. Matter has been given infinite fertility, inexhaustible vitality, and, at the same time, a seductive power of temptation which invites us to create as well. In the depth of matter, indistinct smiles are shaped, tensions built up, attempts at form appear. The whole of matter pulsates with infinite possibilities"...My father never tired of glorifying this extraordinary element—matter. "There is no dead matter," he taught us, "lifelessness is only a disguise behind which hide unknown forms of life. The range of these forms is infinite and their shades and nuances limitless"...As my father proceeded from these general principles of cosmogony to the more restricted sphere of his private interests, his voice sank to an impressive whisper, the lecture became more and more complicated and difficult to follow, and the conclusions which he reached became more dubious and dangerous—Schulz, The Street of Crocodiles.* In supreme narrative all objects as images are psychically alive. The extension of any image in time and space in a language is an analytic of animation for the object. There is no unanimated descriptivity in a supreme narrative. No dead things or times words or paragraphs. All registers of language of whatever length are projects of animation bearing their real. Word for word. Figures of accumulation. Tropes of accretion. Turns of amplification toward lividness for the things to be made significant. All vital showing of matter is this kind of arrangement of a telling. All scene of matter told so. Nothing of matter shown or seen so without being told so. Psychic time itself such picture. Or thought not lived. Livid picture held over a time in the integrity of narrative never a-somatic idea. Narrative telling this significance above all. Of the lived idea dramatic intellect the argued matter. The telling of this presenting all showing holding all showing as significant however held in scene all the seen subsumed within such a told of picture of vital matter. No lifelessness. Diegetic reverberation. All this toldness going back to the language of the object. Infusing it. The residue of the object the perceived object a living mental thing. In supreme narrative the aggregation of a time a space of a world of some quality ever contiguity in whatever duration held formed from the animation of the object seen in its language as a focus of psychic distance. In supreme narrative the technical dialectical. All supreme showing told. Mimetic matter living in the inflection of a diegetic voice. Temporal distance voiced. All livid heard form a metaphysics of temporal inflection between the things in their time and the telling of the things. All telling an argument stood so from a diegetic distance. We see it so when we hear it so. This told of object-matter hiding obscuring disclosing in time the logic of necessity between a seen world and its heard language. Supreme narrative of necessity a dialectical superimposition of temporal and psychic distance. That is its analytic. The word found for the picture. Clarity heard. The lifeless inflected. What lifeless matter now lives most seen most heard in a voice all that what is looked-back-upon in the inflected pictoral focus of a temporal-cum-psychic distance. It is analytical. It must be dialectical. More than coordinates. The told-of-object clearly seen at a distance from the telling giving up all psychic residue in its language this itself a metaphor for supreme narrative. Mentality in matter. The residue of this language in narrative gone far beyond naming giving up qualities beyond the appearance of things. In narrative. Knowing nothing in naming but in narrative. Showing only achieved so in the language of something told. The voice of a speaker bringing to life the unseen matter of the named things of narrative. The symbolic. The matter of the narrative so many reverberating images layered in a manner of speaking in no transcription of the ontological real. Transcription a dead act not seeing a thing let alone a significance. Transcription the dead word the dead sentence the dead thing. Appearance of a thing without a quality. A self. It is not a making. No dimension of mind. Exhibition extension of no emotive space. No expressive language great or small. Nothing under the force of mind. Of time. Pressed to another interior view. Forged. Compressed to reveal what is hidden in things places persons. There is much hidden in them. We are trying to find what is hidden in them. There is all story hidden in them. The life of ontic matter. Narrative revelation. The act of discovered story from out of one's animated objects. There is a set that is always to be at hand. It is a generative set. We all have our own however similar set and story. The set and the language which makes them transcend their similar surfaces makes the story dissimilar. This is the project of language. It comes to the page from the psychic space of the object. No days are dead. All are extraordinary. All reverberate in a palpable quality beyond appearance. That is their substance of psychic matter such days. Therein lies their significance. We must find what it is. We have a feeling for it. There are these some few things we return to. Writing is revealing their quality. Writing is the act of generating quality. These things we return to are not ordinary as they appear most ordinary. We return to them in language as immanent things seen anew in actuality. We tell to disclose. We see diegetically. All is shown told. The most inert matter made a quality a psychic mass. This psychic quantity the weight of narrative held across time and place. The dynamic matter of the subject. The phenomenal function of the form. Yet form here ever more a substance than a function. A palpable quantity of psychic-somatic space-time. Not a quantity of pages or paragraphs. Durational space inducted from the page of printed word sentence paragraph. But not reducible to. A supreme narrative not reducible to its parts only to its act of perception as presentation. Its story an act of formal necessity not a causality of elements. Beyond its source of saying its emergence as narrative its ability to be perceived on a page the phenomenology of its form. Sense significance symbol from sensation. Psychic intellection. Not a semblance of life. Living narrative a kind of body-mind in action. The symbolic made actual in the somatic-psychic. Narrators body-minds living in actual significance. However diegetically from the epiphenomenality of the page. From this living speaking space all told and shown so. All matter a metaphysic. A prosody. A prosody a cosmogony. The inflected expressive temporal mortal word a psychic agent a foremost energy a spark in the story of a world and of the selves constrained within it. The force of a mind felt first from the body. The mind's force come of the mortal body wanting a moral reason and finding one out for such objects at hand. The story. The return to such objects at hand and what is hidden in them the story. The mind forcing the disclosure of matter. Well we want to know what is hidden in them such objects. It is an old want. No matter should we come to tell the story of them we have ourselves always wanted. What is now known is what was once wanted. The force of the body for the mind to speak. Story as a dynamic which cannot be reduced to its spoken parts told up driven out of such want of a mind feeling the body. The transcendence from the somatic to the psychic. Abstraction here always an act of desire. Story the composition of want. Story the accumulation of the known and gone things felt. The return in want to what is gone. Yet to be. We want to return to

what is gone and to know it. To keep it. It is us. Self revelation and curiosity of our everyday objects and selves in recollection. We must put them under the hammer to collect
them at all. Once they were in the world. Now they are not.
One does not know that one should preserve some semblance of them until too late. One cannot. Fortunately that
temporal distance between all what is lost and is. Therein the
writing. One may write of them. Pound them once more into
their psychic shape. Make the words for the feeling of that
reminiscent world under some force. Nothing is undertaken
and told as a known thing of the world in a narrative of any
supremacy without such a force of the mind come back again
over things in time in want. Of what was lost. The force
of a mind come over the time of a body is the forming of
a narrative. Recollection preservation as if mortal absolution
of self. The necessity of this temporal distance for aesthetics itself as a moral form. Perhaps once of a true-told history of the self. Self-disclosure. A diegetic life. The actual
presented in all its significance. The force of one mind in an
act of recovery now the drive of a narrative as a set of facts
ideas episodes incidents acts things persons places made significant in the inflected return to their recurrent loss. Con-
stancy of recovery. Elliptical continuity. Telling the significance of things hidden. To be lost until retold. To be retold
if told. Significance must be told. No matter what is known
stand right before us however an object whether held to be of
a loss or not. It is mute. Lost or not now however recovered

and kept in whatever continuity now found before us what is known all what is retrieved to be known known first by the remembered feeling. The remembered feeling of how it is to be known. Nothing is known to be told but by the remembered feeling of how it is to be told. One cannot induce one thing one true seen richly lived thing to be not seeming to be without a motive somatic force of mind remembering feeling to set some thing out in its true time and place in a telling. Remembering-feeling psychic-somatic narrative. Such supreme narrative being on a page in a word the world of the emotive mind animated at last in its somatic return to the spiritualized object. In remembering feeling. In the somatic arrangement of the psychic world we hear the resonance of essential mortal things as if seeing some interior music made for matter. One does not want to lose it. One recovers all in the recurrence of remembering feeling. On a page the inner life of things made visible in the pitch of that language. That language for life. The livid register of a mind's force. More than a singing of surfaces.

ON THE PHENOMENOLOGY
OF A FICTIVE FORM

The ATAVISM of AESTHETIC PRINCIPLE. *In the realm of the mind, on the other hand, what is primitive is so commonly preserved alongside of the transformed version which has arisen from it that it is unnecessary to give instances as evidence. When this happens it is usually in consequence of a divergence in development: one portion (in the quantitative sense) of an attitude or instinctual impulse has remained unaltered, while another portion has undergone further development...Let us try to grasp what this assumption involves by taking an analogy from another field. We will choose as an example the history of the Eternal City. Historians tell us that the oldest Rome was the Roma Quadrata, a fenced settlement on the Palatine...Of the buildings which once occupied this ancient area [w]e will find nothing, or only scanty remains, for they exist no longer...There is certainly not a little that is ancient still buried in the soil of the city or beneath its modern buildings. This is the manner in which the past is preserved in historical sites like Rome. Now let us, by a flight of imagination, suppose that Rome is not a human habitation but a psychical entity with a similarly long and copious past—an entity, that is to say, in which nothing that has once come into existence will have passed away and all the earlier phases of development continue to exist alongside the latest one—Freud, Civilization and Its Discontents.* Again we are getting toward a thesis. An analytic of an aesthetic. Let us reframe our picture some to see in clearer light. We may say that art when it is vital lives outside all representative rules but not outside the phenomenal. In its presentation of a form it may come round rules as artifacts and limits of the deadenedness of a history no matter it be informed by history as a secondary condition. Let us say secondary for now as cause. Experience comes over history. The phenomenal has made living limits for art. Not deadened rules. An unconscious kind of physics is at play in a supreme aesthetic. It is not firstly historical. It is not firstly cultural. It is atavistic. It is analytical. The epiphenomenal from the phenomenal. The psychic from the somatic. The conceptual from the corporeal. The mind is ever of a body. First. Then history. Then culture. A supreme aesthetics has phenomenal limits not representative rules. Living limits. A supreme narrative is a physics of phenomenal presentation. Immanence in epiphenomenal form. Know another thing too. There are only limits to the phenomenal. There are no epiphenomenal limits to the expressive as an act. There are no limits none to the ranging circumscribing expression of a mortal vision. All extension of person place and thing is possible. It is the most important fact of this aesthetics. A supreme aesthetics is a phenomenal form of living limits. Yet its expression in form has no conceptual textual narrative limits. A cosmogonic expansion. The phenomenal not ever bound by the historical as a subject or a style. Rather the other way round. Its extension is as yet and ever unknown in narrative. The living limits as limits are the principle of the extension of all. All story and style come out of such limit. A history of taste all cultural convention subsumed by the atavistic preservation of the limits of actual perception. That is the happy constraint. All that which is inducted from the sensible and mortal body-mind the ground where we shall find the deduction of a supreme aesthetics. The solid ground limit of the bodymind as substantive persistence of form allows the unlimited expression of a supreme form and its story-style language. It is that predicament of the mortal and the felt as a first principle for the extensiveness and expansiveness of an authentic artistic vision of the human actual however abstract or expressive. There are then supreme things to be seen and said. That which is inducted from the actuality of the body-mind not deduced from history as ideology-taste is the ground of our supreme aesthetics. First. However overcome with history ideology taste. Nothing else can be ground with good reason. These persistent atavistic phenomenal limits as principles deduced so and on that solid ground are analytical. All strong art is historical secondarily in its phenomenality of immanent influence. For the act of coming against history is the prosecution of this persistence in a new extension circumscription widening of a truer real. There is no given singular privileged culture at the single point of a principle of aesthetic presentation as atavistic phenomenal form yet culture informs it. Overcomes it. History informs it. Overcomes it. That is the distinction. And there is the battle then to speak the real into being. The authentic practice of any art is the prosecution of the necessarily new in the face of the limits of experience. Within the historical. The cultural. This very constraint of the phenomenon of history and of culture is the aesthetic analytic force for the novel abstraction and extension of picture and language under the somatic-psychic real to make the old story new. It is dialectical. But only the epiphenomenal from the phenomenal. As cause. Experience is never conventional. It is actual. However cultural. Historical. The affects of a supreme art as form and language are aesthetic effects of the sensible real as body and mind. Overcome in culture. Then there is ideology call it taste. Then there is history call it influence. The weight of representation on the actual. The actual as a real remade. There is then influence come across the actual. Call it immanent in a history. Call it a logic. It is. But experience is actual. Experience in a culture in history is actual. The somatic-psychic. A predicament for the self. For aesthetics. We are born into the actual and made historical. Cultural. They so over-determine the actual. Yet the actual remains. Without it no history no culture. No yesterday no tomorrow. No today. The actual remains supreme in such aesthetic practice. We must remember it. Feel it. To represent it. As the world extant to our remembering-feeling in cohesive form in elemental immanence. Of given substance we have never once originally made. Culture will make us a quality. History will make us mean. Yet there is no history in it the actual. No culture in it the actual. As cause. Until become phenomenal experience of the actual in us to us delivered ontologically to it. History and culture have come about us in us from us. The ontic possibilities of perception persist in the actual. Are immanent in the somatic-psychic. We cannot conceive of a delimited perception of sense. What would it be? However unlimited. It would be immanent. But it would ontically precede our capability of possessing it. To perceive of it we would be born into the actuality of it. To see other. We do not have the ontic instrumentation. Yet. We must make the phenomenological point. It is necessarily a dialectical one. One sees what to say. That is true. And one must say too so to see. History binds the actual into significance. Yet now that is story not strict form. And story must be formed. It is dialectical. One must have an object which is a subject in form. Narrative. The reverberation and residue of the necessary object as a significant image. In time. In every actual object made image nothing ordinary in narrative. Or in a lived constrained life. Again and again to return to the object to its residue as an image to what may be phenomenologically symbolically seen with a limit an eye a mind it is to know that what is truly seen in an art is reseen against its material self in experience and made delimited as a subject. Therein an unlimited psychic residue to all objects. The actual is perpetually symbolized. That is the subject of a language aesthetic sight. Of narrative. We touch we taste we hear we see we move within and act through the duration or cessation of objects places persons things times known and seen kept and wanted lost. However said and seen the narrative world is alive so. The presence and the remembrance of psychic-somatic shadow cast within the walls of all rooms so. One sees what to say of the actuality of the object in the abstraction of the eye to the somatic mind and a psychic picture is formed of the transcendent subject put so against the object into image and held. Narrative language forms. Actuality as narrative is now a literary object. What has become as aesthetic epiphenomenal becomes phenomenal as text. Another object. To inflect another somatic-psychic cause. In an act of reception. The world read as text. But not to alter the logic of causality. First cause. Ontic immanence. In supreme narrative aesthetic vision as an abstraction is ever coming to be visionary against the actuality of the ontologically seen. The somatic a ground of the moral. The psychic mortal. Emotic. The visual dramatic. Nothing is now familiar. Or false. Or if familiar not ever ordinary ever extraordinary. The actual of the actual in an art. No longer rooms as rooms. There are no ordinary rooms as rooms. There never have been. The atavistic necessity of picture. Vision held against the known as it is ontically seen. The eye looks out from a feeling. Something is somatically said of the seen. You feel it in the body. Remembering feeling. The landscape can only be known and held psychically. Thing become thingness. No parceled out preformed space in rooms seen already too many times and never once seen. These are the rooms of the never repeatable life. In passing time. The eye makes a language of picture. The prosecution of phenomenological form necessary for supreme narrative. One must hold narrative to such sights. To old sensations. They are novel actual. One lingers in sensible limits. Perhaps one takes one's time. Well why not there has never been enough. One must take it for one's self. There is no clock time for the actual after all. At length one tells some truly of a real in the held time of the somatic-psychic. And no matter the time the consideration for vision as sensation has always been emotional. There is dramatic interest in picture. The consideration for feeling as a somatic want has always been for the good. There is moral interest in sensation. The consideration for sound in language has always been toward mortal sense. That is its music. There is an intellectual interest in every alliteration in sounded syntax the drive of proliferating thought. It is all an aesthetic interest. Put it how you want. A supreme fiction is dialectical. The dramatic the moral the intellectual the aesthetic inducted from the transcendence of the somatic-psychic. From body-mind to categories of narrative interest an analytical phenomenological function of form. Seeing feeling speaking. A supreme fiction sublime effect the affect of the body and mind. Under the influence of history. The source of supreme narrative analytic elements of that immanence made formally explicit in the long view of history in terms of perception. Aesthetics an induction of that allowance of perception and its persistence as form form of persistence. The somatic to the psychic as the transcendence of feeling the world to feelings about the world. Feeling to remembering feeling thinking feeling the world. Stance taken in language traversing a narrative the solipsistic quality of its traversing. The character of its landscape. Character. Quality grounded in a phenomenology of form as persistent possible perception. Possible limits necessary limits. A supreme fiction come into being as a phenomenology of form. All sight and sound made sense through the psychic-somatic mind-body. We see we hear we feel the necessity of an epiphenomenal narrative phenomenologically bound as we ourselves are bound. It is the clarity of that limit as a kind and force put upon narrative as upon ourselves. Visionary arrangement kept in the eye. Somatic argument held palpable in the body. Psychic space charged emotively across all objects. Seeing hearing feeling all a phenomenology of implication for the reader. Scene appearing visionary. Sentences sounding palpably. Objects animated psychically. Now the symbolic a phenomenon. Narrative dynamically moved by the eye and the ear into the mind feeling the emotive force of objects made images. All persons places and things living before one in a book as in a world. The artifice not artificial. No dead space. Pages of perception. Nothing unfelt or unthought. No dead sentences. No lack of circumscribing consciousness for the narrative as for the world. This phenomenology of form ever a circumscribing consciousness living upon the page in the limits of perception. One as lived as the other. One lived as in the other. Livid. In this limit as a ground of the true of what may be uttered of the real by a mortally materialized speaker by this circumscribing consciousness come in narrative as an ever present living force for the integrity of a form held in its expressive quality yet the unlimited come in expression and expansion the language come which cannot be limited in its variety its recurrence its residue no matter the formal binding of the phenomenology but rather expressively unlimited by this palpable mortal limit. There is no end to the deduction of language from the ground of this form as phenomenological proposition just as there is no limit to the creation of placed images and sentences and persons and things made however recognizable singularly dissimilar in symbolization from perception to perception in the apt reorientation of their significance in their relation in their circulation in their duration in their stylized storied world of the never repeatable life but only to the available space and time allotted the art the aesthetic by the vision of the artist. All such art its specific quality yet allowed to be made by the limits of an apt inductive form. And here then too now in the immanence of history as a lineage but not that of taste for it goes the art as a considered quality may only be said to be well made from the comparison of other objects so formed and under such a ground of limit just as a table or a chair may be said to be well made or not by how it works phenomenologically in the world and for a body in some good purpose. The ontology of the made thing then perceived and held as an aesthetic work arriving being the dialectical actuality between the body-mind and its world. So it is with a narrative work fashioned to be a supreme fiction. We are yet the painters who would paint our time cross rock in caves. We are yet persisting of those bodies and minds. We recognize them for us. We know them in their aesthetic. We paint a far greater number of objects in a far greater number of ways yet we paint in those constraints to make the object image. We make our most forceful stances under those constraints. There are no artificial artifices under those mortally persisting constraints. It is an argument for the atavistic persisting sources and elements of a supreme fiction. It is an argument moving back beyond taste. Argument a-conventional hardly critical. Felt to be thought. Somatically theoretical. Psychically over-determined by its own material history. Culture. Yet. This phenomenology of form at the level of perceiving the elements of an art from the proposition of such ground sources is analytical. We are some same old bodies and minds. We are the great experience of the actual. The atavistic. Within the historical the cultural we are lividly animated in our constrained substance. Too long we have forgot we are beyond our times.

However culturally made of them. A happy dilemma. The phenomenology of form cutting across all history taste convention. But not without it. We have not got out of history. We have forgotten the whole history. There are atavistic limits to the body-mind. They are not ideological. They are ontological. Seeing feeling thinking acting remembering this form visionary somatic psychic form. We are the great experience of the actual and its force put into the practice of an art. It is a rudimentary aesthetics. The sublime comes of it. What is most true of form is within us. We must turn in to it. Now we have ink and paper in our hand. Now we read in our ontic eye. Ear. All is to be seen heard sounded out. Felt remembered phenomenally. And we cannot see or hear or taste or touch or smell one thing but paper and ink. We see hear taste touch smell all things of the supreme narrative world epiphenomenally. Remembering feeling. That recurrence of the real. The actual remade aesthetically phenomenal. In the reception of the literary experience. That experience from form existing in narrative in epiphenomenal phenomena as a transcendent experience. An aesthetic act of supreme perception. The phenomenal transcendent to the epiphenomenal turned to the aesthetic of a fictive form. Experienced. Grounded perception. This atavism of the aesthetic. The livid descent of it. We are the great experience of the actual. The life informs the work. What is most true of form is within us. We must turn in to it.

BOOK TWO

IT MUST CHANGE

ON INFLUENCE
AS A LOGIC OF HISTORY

HISTORY against EXPERIENCE or SIGNIFICANCE. *riverrun, past Eve and Adam's, from swerve of shore to bend of bay, brings us by a commodious vicus of recirculation back to Howth Castle and Environs. Sir Tristram, violer d'amores, fr'over the short sea, had passencore rearrived from North Armorica on this side the scraggy isthmus of Europe Minor to wielderfight his penisolate war: nor had topsawyer's rocks by the stream Oconee exaggerated themselves to Laurens County's gorgios while they went doublin their mumper all the time: nir avoice from afire bellowsed mishe mishe to tauftauf thuartpeatrick: not yet, though venissoon after, had a kidscad buttended a bland old isaac: not yet, though all's fair in vanessy, were sosie sesthers wroth with twone nathandjoe. Rot a peck of pa's malt had Jhem or Shen brewed by arclight and rory end to the regginbrow was to be seen ringsome on the aquaface. The fall... of a once wallstrait oldparr is retaled early in bed and later on life down through all Christian minstrelsy. The great fall of the offwall entailed at such short notice the pftischute of Finnegan, erse solid man, that the humptyhillhead of humself promptly sends and unquiring one well to the west in quest of his tumptytumtoes: and their upturnpikepointandplace is at the knock out in the park where oranges have been laid to rust upon the green since devlinsfirst loved livvy*—Joyce, *Finnegans Wake*. If one were ontologically original one would be incomprehensible. There is a way to read Joyce. We cannot be original in the original sense. There is no actual originality. Joyce has his Milton. Milton has his. It is not our lateness. We have always been too late. Fortunately that is our catalyst. Originality newness difference relation context comparison extension. Not ever Originality. Originality is an historical claim not an ontological state. If we say one is original we have made an historical statement not a claim about the actual. There are rational aspects to the idea of originality. They are not found in the actual. That actual. They are historical. They are of a material culture. Contextual judgment not of the actual. There is nothing rational about the state of the actual. Genius and the original follow from the historical. Nothing follows from the actual. But in perception. It is bare in its real. The very readability of a literature is an act of influence as a logic of history. Whatever its originality it is extant in relation to history. Bound to some given as a claim for a difference. Influence and originality as artistic acts inextricably bound. And out of the actual one moves always against this logic. One must speak for one's self. One sees and feels some thing. One is present against the given. All representation. One makes a word a stand against the given. And in doing so creates the novel out of the historical. History orients and signifies. Originality seeks the actual for the word. The given word ordinary not the actual. One speaks out of the actual. The one real act speaking. But one only means in relation. Only a quality of newness known in relation. The actual symbolized. It must change. And the actual is never different significantly. And the actual never ordinary yet the same. We do not want the ordinary. We want the actual. Yet in recollection significance. History comes across the actual to signify. Supreme narratives move significantly so. Significance the residue of the historical binding the actual. There must be story. We want story new. Any newness. There is no new story. We are the same now a long time. The same must be different. The actual is new. Yet the same. This story the same but different. The actual ever new and always the same. Story generalized in such sameness. Yet each instance of individual experience new real true different unrepeatable and substantively divided from history. The actual moving against the logic of history as influence. The self ever gaining its own space. There is the never repeatable speaking subject. A voice takes up a language. It is a somatic language. One feels all what is at stake. One speaks out of the actual stands against the historical. This act itself one of literature. The logic of influence produces producing a counter resistance to a-contextualized a priori signification. Against it one speaks in singular resistance. One sees feels speaks one's self no one else has. Story generalizes this. Language particularizes this. That is the somatic stance. We hear an argument against the world against all others who have spoken of it so. Said it so. Well one must speak for one's self. Each word is an act of the actual. The self is the history of remembering feeling thinking. Acting. We want the actual. Our actual. We must remember. We remember ourselves. In our acts retold. This distance between the actual and the recollected as experience the temporal distance of significance. The time of symbol-led telling. Inflected language. The story is the same. The stakes. The language an act of difference. Style the shadow of a personality. The utterance of the never again repeatable subject character narrator heard strongly against the given. Poetry emotion recollected not exactly in tranquility but in distance. Writing itself actual expressive ontological act only made so in a temporal logic of the past. The influence of what has come before one the very generative logic of the creative present. One wants to get out of it. One cannot get out of it. Influence. One should not want to. One wants to. One cannot. The only way out is through. One writes. The story is the same. Language made against history as the vital novel difference between the mortal predicament of the lived individual experience of the actual and the deadened finishedness of history. Significance arrives in the act of this temporally bound logic. One resists the over-determination of history. One must if to speak at all. All supreme narrative has. All supreme narrative a claim for the actual over the historical. The actual as it is spoken now against the historical as it is known. One steps outside convention to the true. A claim for the individual as a somatic mortal source of speaking the new in the face of the same old end. The stake-story ever the same. The story ends the same. Yet one argues authentically against it. One finds one's voice in the continuous face of the familiar-known end. The language of what is at stake the expression of this our fundamental ground mortal constraint. That true subject the elevation of a style. The somatic-cum-psychic word a voice placed against the given. There is a style. Style mortal personality. The history of literature is the history of personality. Not representation. Mimetic-diegesis. Presentation against the given. This narrative means against the end. Expression subsuming history in the psychic-somatic act of speaking against what is too given and all done. All has already been said. Yet we ourselves feel. The actual stands and remains. It is the solid ground for all new word. So it is one speaks. One speaks so and in such a way. We are of palpable body and mind. The actual subsumes the historical in the act. No matter the logic of history as influence remain. Words are bound by it. The actual subsumes the historical in the act of speaking as most actual yet. What is spoken of so only means in the relation. It is dialectical. The analytical relation is transformation. What is bound unbound. Influence a geometric logic of history. All supreme narrative significantly transformatively happily bound by influence no matter if telling otherwise. Influence the first prime logic of literary history. It is the most productive logic for a history of a literature. It is an orienting logic. It is an extending logic. It is a discriminating accruing transforming logic. In the face of the historical the want of originality as the want of nothing given to the actual so to signify the new and yet to signify in some pure state of quality as if a speaking god is contradictory. No matter we speak godlike. For if pure there is no teleology. No transcendence or transformation. If literature a kind of pure once-spoken science. Nothing would be significant. One would not be able to read Joyce. One would not be able to read. We speak godlike against all come against an end. The ground of our speaking opens up all again. We read ourselves out of what all has and will come again. Nothing is for once and all quieted in some Originality. Mortal narrative cannot have that ontological actual as an original originality beyond the historical but for in its own phenomenal act of reframing of the world in its form as a difference a newness and this yet only in historical relation or nothing significant of good. The storied real a moral mortal one. That its narrative project and its constraint. The sacred subject of some supreme secular narrative. The fictive phenomenal as a supreme epiphenomenal form signifying out of the actual made the human in remembrance. It is an old aesthetic. It is the beginning of aesthetic. Somatic-psychic abstraction of the real into picture storied constrained to significance by remembrance history. That is narrative. A supreme narrative extends that actual and constraint. In a book. In a book in a history. In a book in a history in an actuality. In a life. To close the distance between the actual and the book. The life. Narrative as a supreme art moves presents enacts itself somatically psychically phenomenologically in its aesthetic form in this human gap we ourselves have closed in our own true living between sensation and sense if it is to be vital organic authentic art. A supreme art performs its want of actuality and its preservation as life against such preserved influence arriving already done and lived up to make it mean to make it change. It must change. It does not want history. It wants life. The strong act of its phenomenal unfolding is to be beyond history as form. It is to live. The quality of its language at its most authentic is somatic-psychic abstraction of the phenomenal into form. It is of livid form. That actual first. Its form at its most authentic first a phenomenology of form. However overcome in history. A supreme aesthetics must be abstracted from the body-mind and grounded so. Yet narrative's ability to mean always a relation of the historical. Its ability to be read. But one must see the critical dialectical difference between the analytical actual and the historical. So put. Read. There is a difference between the ground of this aesthetics and the narrative's relation as a work to the history of a literature. The aesthetic as a form abstracted from the persisting body-mind stands a-historical. Its phenomenological ground is analytical. An analytic of the actual. Its supreme aesthetic stands in dialectical relation of history to the persistence of the act of perception. Or nothing first seen and felt beyond the already given the historical as the given. First ontic cause. No matter the narrative as a work inducted from this aesthetic as a-historical form stands in direct dialectical relation to history. The narrative a spoken driven expression-spark a propelled act of singular personality undertaken most sublimely in phenomenal form and in swerving averring resistance to all other given word for the world. No last word for the world. Expressive vital life self-force proliferating in the face of history. The moral demand of self for its own word. No matter its significance forms most powerfully in direct relation to what it will speak against when speaking for itself as the word for the world. In correcting. Extending. Widening. It has taken up the historical and the actual. History as influence allows us to read it morally when so mortally formed. Influence as a logic of history allows us to read actuality significantly. No matter atavistic phenomenal form as vital spark allow a new unheard language. We hear in relation to what has been heard. A moral and mortal language is made and means against history risen out of the constant and unchanging atavism of our supreme aesthetic. It cannot change. It must change.

ON THE AESTHETICS
OF INFLUENCE

The STYLIZATION of the SAME OLD real THING. *Sometimes in reading, sometimes in thinking, sometimes in realising, sometimes in a kind of a way in feeling, knowing repeating knowing always everything is repeating, knowing that there will be going on living is saddening. Sometime then in reading, in realizing anything, a little sometimes in feeling something it is saddening to be thinking, feeling, realizing that always everything, is repeating, that sometime some one is a young one and that now some one is in their middle living and that now some one is an old one and sometimes it is a queer feeling in one this and then not anything, not writing, reading, dying, being a dead one, living, being a young one, being one is a real thing inside in one then and always then it is certain that always every one is living and every one has their being in them and every one is feeling thinking knowing something and always then it is certain that every one is like some other one and everything is existing and it is saddening then and existing is not a real thing then to some one feeling then every one as existing and being themselves inside them and some one being like some one and each one being either a young one or a middle aged one or an old one and sometime then this is a little a dreary thing and sometimes then it is a very queer thing and mostly then it is all then something and mostly then it is certain that everything is existing and mostly then it is inside in some one that not anything is a real thing, that it is dreary to be writing—Stein, The Making of Americans.* If one should write a book of a particular kind at a particular time in history one might well want to say a few words about it just as if even about one's own child once brought into being and set out into the world to make its own way. And as with children there is ever much to say. There is all to say. All to go on at length about. Yet one knows not really what to properly say of such a thing to another. There is something presumptuous and indiscrete about such pronouncements of all things that come to live on their own. Talk at bottom too intimate. Revelations nevertheless mistaken. For what such a book does it can say itself and be taken at its word or not. But even as one might not want to too truly with particular children one might say something of how a book came into being as when telling a general kind of family history. And as with such a family history the ancestry or rather more properly the genealogy of this or that book—to become more precise about one's predecessors if not parentage—is ever a thing of interest not only to others but indeed to one's self. That is what one wants. As if that lineage could in the end tell you something about the very life going on before you now in such pages at hand in this world in these hands in these days at hand in this book. Or in one written in relation to it. It can. It cannot. Yes it is a kind of descendency one speaks from without. Or rather one speaks from within out. For such lineage true imagined ontological or epiphenomenal it is a kind of frame for all one's way of speaking and why. For one is both necessarily from the beginning with it and against it. For one must have it and one must be rid of it. It is this that one must come to speak round it out of it. Or to think so to get from out it. We will say there is an aesthetics of influence necessary for supremacy. We will say just as in the history of sciences there is in the history of aesthetics as in a life or one would like to yet think so and we will a widening act of circumscription one holding a claim to a truer statement about the real of person place and thing. No matter true or not only extending this truer true in relation. The world is no different in substance. History is simply longer. There is a stylization of the same old real thing. That is simply to say once more in repeating one wants one's own words. One wants nothing once and for all given for the world and for one's self. Too much is given. One is already too in love with one's own voice. That voice is the world. That voice is not the world. There is this history. There is no history. There is a voice. And there is a history. And one may only now speak in such a voice truly the act in itself of which is never historical from out of history. It is dialectical. There is history come round any and all voice. There is a world a history a voice each come one round the other. It is a kind of fight. For better or for worse words are born of it. And the words come and go for each writer of the same old real thing as when a child comes at last one way or the other to go on from a mother or a father. To go once and for all from the house. No matter what all is come and gone be the same. All repeating. No matter the unrepeatable life. All has long been no different. All must be stylized. To speak. To speak what is at stake. All that story in style. All this new real. One's own word. For the old. One must get out of the house for good. So it is with the books one has read once loved and left. Yet once loved even if no longer they cannot be so easily left. Lost. And they are not. Do you think they can be? They cannot. Do not think they can. For they cannot. And even should you forget and you should want to—to want to is the thing—should you you would not then yet ever know now one thing as when without all parent good or bad about your nascent expressive self sent into the world to make it change it. You would know nothing but experience. Or rather the fullness of sheer experience. And would not even know it. A kind of paradig-matic false consciousness of self-authoring of how one has truly come to one's expressively accountable aesthetic self. Fortunately you cannot get out so cleanly no matter if you should want to. You should want to. Be careful if you should want to too badly. Cleanly. For you would have not one real thing to say and no good way to say it. We are coming to a subject. We must stylize the same old real thing against what we have long heard whether liked loved necessary or not. There is an aesthetic of influence. We refigure the real against our heard history no matter of a life or a book. But do you not want to speak so and in such-a-way? What is your argument against the world? Against books? You know that is the somatic-aesthetic question. All comes of it. Yes happily luckily this necessary leaving that you cannot ever get out of this ever going and not getting gives up all for one to say. Is the rupture of a real. There is thankfully then no end to what must be said. Reseen as real. We are happy for history. Though it is the one real thing we do not want. In strong remaking. We want it gone. Going on out against from one's most given words framed acts is a speaking aesthetics. It is a going made manifest most widely in getting round against them from out them such words and acts and words as acts. The very acute and conscious turning of the self from one given word to another world. Now an informed oriented aptly related readable extensional aesthetics. There are no clean breaks. You do not want them. Any. Remember that. You do not need to do a thing but remember. Fortunately you must go but you cannot get out. Only the self-authoring madly prophetic may do that. Creatively incomprehensible in outdistancing history to circumvent it. To eclipse the actual. The human. Some godlike original too soon undone in an as yet unintelligible language. Writing is glacial endurance. Human hardness. History frames being. We remember that and do not want that. Nor to forget that. And that is the situated center of supreme speaking. The situated constrained unfreed mortal self in search of its apt and wise own first sustaining necessary word for the world. Caught in solitude and silence. For the world such confinement and constraint the hard weight of history as of adamantine stone held to suppress the speaker's freed rising word. One works one's words strongest in the lack of originary freedom. One's moral and mortal weight transcended in felt force from the actual to be cast into one's own style. One battles to be heard. To be new and true. One's hardest history become the stylization of the same old real thing. History too remembered. To be ransacked. Razed. But never quelled. Stopped up. It is an aesthetic source. Its influence for story is ever to be stylized. Restylized. Form to be epiphenomenally rearranged. In style the real sounded anew. The world risen in new extending form. No matter phenomenally the same. After all who know how the realized world should sound and look in epiphenomenal rearrangement. However recognizable as long as mortally sounded. Seen. In material form now cast in a resembling shape upon a page beneath some one or another motive hand with particular chisel. Style chisel. A spoken word turned. There are simple spoken words become the beautiful or sublime of a life of a book. Turned. To find one's real style in a necessary speaking spark of a singular self so to constrain the long familiar story of selves in a word not yet once heard so. To extend it to widen it however particular.

History of the same old real thing made new. Out of a page or two the pleasure the terror the human and inhuman worlds and words come truly strongly into their unfolding being. Another emerging real recognized for the aestheticized actual. Stylization cosmogony. The world once and for all made in godlike voice. Of a style. Syntax. Yes the elevation of language comes too readily at times. But how one will love the sound of it. If not all its implications. And why not speak so if one is to speak of all that is to be lost. We should tell it true that we are a long time now ever to be freed of history. Not ever ordinary history. Ever a kind of familial history. A kind of house one must simply go from. It is simply that one must go. And one cannot get wholly out. One might say in Romantic and Longinian senses that there there is the very landscape and the figured source of the stylization of story. One's necessity of going from of ever eclipsing aesthetic familial influence which has allowed us first to see the world and in such a way. There in going the generation of the expressive history of the mortal subject-self in search of necessary word in one's going. Of sublime word for the solipsistic self in going. In the going one speaks. It is a turning. Itself a transport. Mortal. Liberating. Delimiting. Defining. What it is to see and to hear and to feel what it is to go. There is newness in the feeling. The turning away. Troping in the real travel off. In that first loss of home. The self most found. Generative loss. Freed in reflective distance. The opening of a language. A feeling for a first necessary statement of the self and what is significant. Once gone. I tell you truly one must have one's proper loss in sight so to speak to begin to speak. Or in speaking see it so. Living itself is enough to get it. One has always got it. One might say there is no true word without this Subject-Loss then expressed in the logic of a feeling. Remembering feeling. Going off you might look everywhere in the world for it. You will not find it in such a classically mimetic way. It is diegetically lit in one whether of a narrator or a writer as a kind of low consuming fire. Continual combustion. Remembrance of the actual formed in some old atavistic rekindling of all what has passed. Held to the presently passing. That temporal diegetic distance. Now there you will find it in you in the actual a rich residue so many burning coals of a reflective soul so to speak should you look down in the darkest corners of such feeling. Remembering feeling. We find our surest speaking so and form it in such reflection. Narrative recollection. Knowing nothing of aestheticized self but in narrative. We are telling ourselves. Stylizing selves against the prior and the gone. Aesthetics in turned relation to history. An aesthetics of influence where houses books fathers mothers friends loves we have turned from gone off from in some strict sense frame us in circulation. The remembrance of relation. In the freed dynamics of that turn there come up the spark of our own found word. We find our style in all the old somatic psychic constraints of the actual aesthetically rekindled in every turning away from the historical. We want in supreme narrative the expressive transcendence of the essential life to the page. Our life. Then there is history. There is the house one has come from. There are all the given words one has heard for the world. Looks long seen in the cold in the going light. There is the same old real thing. These rooms. That talk. Those books. All picture long heard so and in such a way. All the priority of an overcoming literature. In the going the turn away the books one has read will come to read like a genealogical good father's guide and directive. Yet they are a constraint. Too like a mother's loving word to come and to stay to home in the house. They are ever a constraint. You want them. You need them. You must have them. You cannot be without them. You leave them. You cannot leave them. You do. You cannot have any longer what is simply given. Yet what is simply given must be had. It is prior. It is history. We want experience. It is a paradoxical journey such a novel way of living and speaking turning remembering and feeling. You deviate and go. There is generation. There is the figure of the subject. Self. Going far off in the turning. In going to forget all what has been said and seen yet remembering to say so. No you cannot get wholly out of the house. You should want to remembering that you cannot no matter how you are to happily forget. To strongly turn away. For who wants one day to be found walking bereft in some self-imposed poverty quietly along the barren road too newly naked with no adequate and necessary provision at last for one once truly gone on alone and now too quieted in one's own very close-kept self on that long wandering journey off to where and how? One does not want that diasporatic wandering poverty. Not even when one is to find at last one's true way if there should be one. One wants a literature within which to richly turn. I will tell you the happy thing about such parentage for good or worse is that it is always to be in question no matter it truly exists as almost nothing else exists. The question of it the doubt to one of its defining is enough. It is ever now in question no matter one knows so very well and is ever to recall and to be happy or not at the thought of it what house one has stepped from out of over what boot-trammeled doorstep to all that is and is to be said and seen once turned out from after. As in a literature the whole history of a house and of those long dead who have lived good years in it luckily remains yet at hand to have and to hold to keep as a good guide and companion however how far off from home at last travelled and kept most in such books as those you cannot ever get out from once read kept as one cannot ever keep one's own few mortal loves lost if ever one has no matter if remembered or forgot. And others are ever to come. Be. Go. All houses are yet to be built and to be gone from. All changes. It must change. Nothing is different. All is different. One stylizes the same old real thing.

ON NORMATIVE GENERATION
AND TRANSFORMATION

AESTHETICS of INFLUENCE or the MAKING of a MOD-
ERN AMERICAN STYLE. *The first thing that happened
when we were back in Paris was Hemingway with a letter
of introduction from Sherwood Anderson. I remember very
well the impression I had of Hemingway that first afternoon.
He was an extraordinary good-looking young man, twenty
-three years old...So Hemingway was twenty-three, rather
foreign looking, with passionately interested, rather than interesting eyes. He sat in front of Gertrude Stein and listened
and looked. They talked then, and more and more, a great
deal together...Stein went over all the writing he had done
up to that time. He had begun the novel that it was inevi-
table he would begin and there were the little poems afterwards printed by McAlmon in the Contact Edition. Gertrude
Stein rather liked the poems, they were direct, Kiplingesque,
but the novel she found wanting. There is a great deal of
description in this, she said, and not particularly good description. Begin over again and concentrate, she said...He
and Gertrude Stein used to walk together and talk together*

a great deal. One day she said to him...If you keep on doing newspaper work you will never see things, you will only see words and that will not do, that is of course if you intend to be a writer. Hemingway said he undoubtedly intended to be a writer...was very earnestly at work making himself a writer. Gertrude Stein never corrects any detail of anybody's writing, she sticks strictly to general principles, the way of seeing what the writer chooses to see, and the relation between that vision and the way it gets down. When the vision is not complete the words are flat, it is very simple, there can be no mistake about it, so she insists. It was at this time that Hemingway began the short things that afterwards were printed in a volume called In Our Time. One day Hemingway came in very excited about Ford Madox Ford and the Transatlantic. We had heard that Ford was in Paris, but we had not happened to meet. Gertrude Stein had however seen copies of the Transatlantic and found it interesting but had thought nothing further about it. Hemingway came in then very excited and said that Ford wanted something of Gertrude Stein's for the next number and he, Hemingway, wanted The Making of Americans to be run in it as a serial and he had to have the first fifty pages at once. Gertrude Stein was of course quite overcome with her excitement at this idea, but there was no copy of the manuscript except the one that we had had bound. That makes no difference, said Hemingway, I will copy it and it was printed in the next number of the Transatlantic. So for the first time a piece of the

monumental work which was the beginning, really the be-
ginning of modern writing, was printed, and we were very
happy. Later on when things were difficult between Gertrude
Stein and Hemingway, she always remembered with grati-
tude that after all it was Hemingway who first caused to be
printed a piece of The Making of Americans. She always
says, yes sure I have a weakness for Hemingway. After all
he was the first of the young men to knock at my door and he
did make Ford print the first piece of The Making of Ameri-
cans. I myself have not so much confidence that Hemingway
did do this...Gertrude Stein and Sherwood Anderson are very
funny on the subject of Hemingway. The last time that Sher-
wood was in Paris they often talked about him. Hemingway
had been formed by the two of them and they were both a
little proud and a little ashamed of the work of their minds.
Hemingway had one moment, when he had repudiated Sher-
wood Anderson and all his works, written him a letter in
the name of american literature which he, Hemingway, in
company with his contemporaries was about to save, tell-
ing Sherwood just what he, Hemingway thought about Sher-
wood's work, and, that thinking, was in no sense complimen-
tary. When Sherwood came to Paris Hemingway naturally
was afraid. Sherwood as naturally was not...But what a
book, they both agreed, would be the real story of Heming-
way, not those he writes but the confessions of the real Er-
nest Hemingway...And then they both agreed that they have
a weakness for Hemingway because he is such a good pu-

pil. He is a rotten pupil, I protested. You don't understand, they both said, it is so flattering to have a pupil who does it without understanding it, in other words he takes training and anybody who takes training is a favourite pupil... he looks like a modern and he smells of the museums. And that is Hemingway, he looks like a modern and he smells of the museums. But what a story that of the real Hem, and one he should tell himself but alas never will...there is the career, the career. But to come back to the events that were happening. Hemingway did it all. He copied the manuscript and corrected the proofs. Correcting proofs is, as I said before, like dusting, you learn the values of the thing as no reading suffices to teach it to you. In correcting these proofs Hemingway learned a great deal and he admired all that he learned It was at this time that he wrote to Gertrude Stein saying that it was she who had done the work in writing The Making of Americans and he and all his had but to devote their lives to seeing that it was published...In the meantime McAlmon had printed the three poems and ten stories of Hemingway and William Bird had printed In Our Time and Hemingway was getting to be known. He was coming to know Dos Passos and Fitzgerald and Bromfield and George Antheil and everybody else and Harold Loeb was once more in Paris. Hemingway had become a writer...In those early days Hemingway liked all his contemporaries except Cummings. He accused Cummings of having copied everything, not from anybody but from somebody. Gertrude Stein who had been much impressed by The Enormous Room said that Cummings did not copy, he was the natural heir of the New England tradition with its aridity and its sterility, but also with its individuality. They disagreed about this. They also disagreed about Sherwood Anderson. Gertrude Stein contended that Sherwood Anderson had a genius for using a sentence to convey a direct emotion, this was in the great american tradition, and that really except Sherwood there was no one in America who could write a clear and passionate sentence. Hemingway did not believe this, he did not like Sherwood's taste. Taste has nothing to do with sentences, contended Gertrude Stein...So then Hemingway's career was begun...At this time Hemingway was preparing his volume of short stories to submit to publishers in America...he brought the manuscript he intended sending to America. He handed it to Gertrude Stein. He had added to his stories a little story of meditations and in these he said that The Enormous Room was the greatest book he had ever read. It was then that Gertrude Stein said, Hemingway, remarks are not literature...And if he could only tell his own story. In their last conversation she accused him of having killed a great many of his rivals and put them under the sod. I never, said Hemingway, seriously killed anybody—Stein, The Autobiography of Alice B. Toklas. We are making in turning off from out against. We are writing making out against. Of whatever form and language we hear most clearly narrative as a site of style-form located in a history of style-form. It means against history. It is made against a history. We hear narrative clearly as a stylistic formal stance in a history of influence and reception-reaction making aesthetic. The normative generative analytic is one of a thetic taking up. An antithetical rejecting. A swerving correcting. A transformational extending. An aesthetic of influence. Taking turning correcting extending. This analytic logic of aesthetic reception is not of a time but across time against a writer writers against a book against books a literature against literature. Making literature. It is normative. Normative in a time horizon of textually received tradition and solipsistic selves. All what has come most familiarly across us as priorness as if already our own word spoken for all the experience of the world before us circumscribing us as if in such parentage such priority the real real already once and for all said and received. Too taken. It is. It is taken and turned. Well we want our own word for the world. World-word. We will write it. At last. True. All self-regard in self speaking-making. World-making. Self-regard in recognition. In tradition. Recognition. Value. Comparison. Singular invention. The history of aesthetics as such is not to be understood in form but influence. Comparative form. Influence as a normative aesthetic of style-form. In the making of the solipsistic self. *The Making of Americans* as a short sketch of about thirty-five pages was written in 1903. Most of the book was written between 1906-08. The last section was written in 1911. The book started out as a history of Stein's family. Then through character analyses and charts "became the history of every kind of every individual human being." In 1924 Hemingway recopied the beginning of the manuscript for Stein and corrected the proofs for the type-set first fifty pages or so. The book to become now a historical progenitor of a descent of Modern American writing. That family history. Hemingway was working on *In Our Time*. Writing out. He was taking up and turning. Writing out against. Correcting. Extending. He was circumscribed by Stein. He was all taken up. Ford Madox Ford published Stein's first recopied part written out by Hemingway in April 1924 in *Transatlantic Review* along with a piece by Joyce. The entire book was published in France by Contact Editions in 1925. Then published in America in 1926. *In Our Time* was published in 1925. The one book *The Making of Americans* a grand analytical abstraction of the real. The other *In Our Time* a concrete lyrical compression of the real. Each moving in stylized antithesis to the other. Form. But we hear the one in the other. They are very familiar with one another. There is a stylistic genetic genealogy even as between the sound and sight of a mother and son. The one calling to the other even in their own dissimilar book in a familiar voice as if telling how to come best to home. At the level of the sentence the writing moves under the drive of similar declarative syntax limited diction well-placed repetition to embody emotion. No matter the one be concretizing and the other abstracting. And there is Anderson. There is the straight clarity of Anderson's localized things pictured close to one and one's emotion in the familiar thing at hand. We hear Anderson as if hearing a father speaking as a good guide for feeling pictured. It is clear. It is compressed. We hear it in Hemingway. We can find it in Faulkner. However extended. Another son of Anderson. In Hemingway and too in Faulkner in each clarity of emotion of close picturing of the psychic-somatic real of the actual we hear the simplicity of diction of person place and thing of *Winesburg, Ohio*. Emotion pictured. No matter how it has been turned. Corrected. Extended. We hear the emotive incremental accruing repetition of Stein. There are familial favorite sentences. Words in common. These narratives are of a kind at the level of the sentence when carrying the phenomenal of the actual. All to present on the page a true somatic-psychic space. Yet antithetical in project and picture. Form. Striving to be other in overt scope. They are each wanting to surround the world in their own way. No matter we hear the one in the other. We hear the one come on in the other. No matter they must be different and are. And are because they must. One finds one's forms for the stylized subject of the self no matter the aesthetics of influence. Under the influence. One must to generate any thing of worth. Solipsism reformed. Hemingway has his wound. Stein hers. Anderson Faulkner theirs. It is enough to live. It is. Unrepeatable never again experience. Yet one writes within history. We look out for ourselves between the actual and the historical. We want experience. History tells us what significantly means. Comparatively. Humanly. No matter should we reject it. Out of a transformational lineage there is strong writing. Formed in it. Stein writes. Anderson reads Stein and writes. Hemingway reads Stein. Reads Stein through Anderson writing reading Stein and writes. Faulkner reads Stein through reading Anderson writing reading Stein and writes. Hemingway copies Stein out writing her into him transforming reading Anderson reading Stein. Hemingway and Faulkner reading Anderson reading Stein writing resist one another formally estranged brothers reading through Turgenev and Milton Twain and Proust. Americanism. Continentalism. Emotion becomes an architecture. The mortal. Moral. Form-style. Stein syllogizes mortal moral emotion in her sheer abstraction. Anderson in his synoptic locale. Faulkner in his mythic ranging real. Hemingway in his lyrical concrete. Moral allegory all. All mortal emotion form of all what is at stake stylized in some large difference. True feeling made in the same different thing. No matter what surrounding architecting framing form they each know in their narrative vision there is no feeling for the thing at-its-realist at its most true but in the stylized presentation of the phenomenal declared and written out so. Singularly. Definitively. However stylized against one another there is the authoritative act of strong declaration. There is always declaration. When in doubt declaration. Ever declaration as presentation. That stance for the claiming sentence. The true put to the real. In each the strength of declaration beneath all difference when the world must be written out. They write out the world. As though once and for all. That stance genetic in the sentence. Replicated in whatever variant of diction or distance. Duration. We hear it. We hear it cannot be otherwise. No matter sentences be then unowned. As kind. Syntax. As if any one writer could own the act of declaration as a personal style this very atavistic rhetoric of the self this expression as old as the first realized assertion of the self in the face of the world and all others come round one in it. Where in itself this act of declaration a kind of first art born of one's very abstraction from the world in order to order it reorder it in the necessity of self. Declaration. Speaking. Voice. The point of view where all is at stake. All is at stake for the self in the world. Of it comes language. Language comes of a point of view at stake. Pages of perception. It is this analytic. It is an assertion that as a kind is a power of expression reaching past convention. Far on past the contemporary. The escape from stockness. To lividness. Vital form. Writing out the life. Life powering rhetoric. Aesthetic. Normative. Toward supreme fiction. Narrative stylization to bear the real. Palpable form. All sentences bearing the real to the page. No dead sentences. The Moderns in American literary history writing that out for good good at writing this life into their formal kinds their narrative their sentences. It is one of the Modern kinds. It is not original or owned. It is true. However received. It is an exercise in the phenomenology of form. The practice of psychic-somatic presentation. In that declarative act possessing livid authenticity. It is one of the straight acts of the self. It is a deceptively true art. It is simple rudimentary. Atavistic. Genetic. It comes of supreme proliferating aesthetics. Descendency. One not unfamiliarly wide in unrecognizable qualitative difference in such a family of relational formal features however each gone far off from one another in their stylized taking turning correcting extending. Familial. Singular. Individual. Differentiating. In the aesthetics of influence there there is all the claim of difference. There is ever alteration as variation. But style not once and for all freed to its own self-begotten end. Not of another family. There is a return. There yet at the level of word and sentence the similar. Trait tones. If we listen. And when we listen we hear this familial syntax this diction this repetition recurrence in the essential emotional sites of this particular family in their sounded sites of the real as if a heard traditional music of the Modern no matter the difference of literary project. We hear a Modern American harmonics. In particular works and between particular writers. Those that have stylized the actual toward the true in a-way-of familial speaking. Familially estranging speaking. It is complicated. Incestuous. Influenced. Individual. Inventive. Dialectical. Stylization the harmonic complication of the melody-motif of some same old story. Song. But one written out now as though at last true. Sung real. By one who knows now how to speak the real so to take up and to alter once and for all. Not now the same old story. True felt picture refocused reformed reseen in a necessary new sounding. Claim harmonically sounded. Inflected with a whole history of complicating influence. Harmonics complicates. Story as a style first. The story in the style. World-making in-a-way-of-speaking. A story-style. A personality. The complicating tonality of solipsistic voice. The individuality of the one unrepeatable subject. The experience of a lived life heard on a page. Yet harmonics. A complicated self-singing. No matter history. Out of history. Style the shadow of a personality.

ON THE CIRCUMSCRIPTION
OF THE TRUER REAL

TAKING Up and TURNING AWAY to the NEW TRUE
REAL. *The pictures were exciting and the talk was very
good. She talked, mostly, and she told me about modern pictures and about painters—more about them as people than
as painters—and she talked about her work. She showed me
the many volumes of manuscript that she had written and
that her companion typed each day. Writing every day made
her happy, but as I got to know her better I found that for
her to keep happy it was necessary...that she receive recognition...she had published three stories that were intelligible to anyone. One of these stories, "Melanctha," was
very good and good samples of her experimental writing had
been published in book form...She had such a personality...
She had also discovered many truths about rhythms and the
uses of words in repetition that were valid and valuable and
she talked well about them. But she disliked the drudgery of
revision and the obligation to make her writing intelligible,
although she needed to have publication and official accep-
tance, especially for the unbelievably long book called The*

Making of Americans. This book began magnificently, went on very well for a long way with stretches of great brilliance and then went on endlessly in repetitions that a more conscientious and less lazy writer would have put in the waste basket. I came to know it very well as I got—forced, perhaps would be the word—Ford Madox Ford to publish it in The Transatlantic Review serially, knowing that it would outrun the life of the review. For publication in the review I had to read all of Miss Stein's proof for her as this was work which gave her no happiness. The way it ended with Gertrude Stein was strange enough. We had become very good friends and I had done a number of practical things for her such as getting her long book started as a serial with Ford and helping type the manuscript and reading her proof and we were getting to be better friends than I could ever wish to be. There is not much future in men being friends with great women although it can be pleasant enough before it gets better or worse, and there is usually even less future with truly ambitious women writers—Hemingway, A Moveable Feast. First a taking up. Then a turning away. It is all again about want of originality against an aesthetic of influence. But let us briefly talk again of form first. Of some supreme aesthetics. All that which epiphenomenally allows the perception of the work as a phenomenal form. All that which allows the acuteness of actuality on a page. A correspondence of the real. All that which places us in a palpable mortally seen and felt real in a book. Of whatever abstraction. All that which allows an authentic speaking to take place as an act of personal style. All stylizing the real. There is a history of stylizing the real. The aesthetics of influence a history of style. It happens between books. It is ontologically found in books as a cup is found in a cupboard. Neither this aesthetic of influence nor our supreme aesthetic of the phenomenal can be an aesthetic of taste. They are each analytical. They are of a contiguous ontic time not of a time. They are of a contiguous somatic-psychic hearing-speaking time not of a calendar time. The one is of the body-mind. The other is of experience speaking against history. The one is between the body-mind and the actual. The other is between a solipsistic personality and the history of a literature. The aesthetics of influence the history of style generating style. Form form. One hears a true thing and takes it up. Swerving correcting extending of style-form widening solipsistic stance. Correcting extending of style-form come across the epiphenomenal real between books reading the real in such-away. It is the figure of one writing turned in a claim to stand in position in relation to another however strong as somehow incomplete. Yet in genealogical relation. In descendency. The prior one has allowed the stance of the other in a history of writing. Reading. One must originate one's own words. One refigures the relationship. Writes one's self. Sees a wider true in accounting for one's self. Sees a wider true now in accounting for one's self. This refiguring as aesthetic act stood between books stood so against one another as a completion is nevertheless come

necessarily from out across the too persisting sense of an already completed literary history. One learns how to speak in
relation to its sense of completion by reading it. One learns
how to speak in some widening held to be truer voice for
the real in relation to reading it. To recomplete it. One finds
one's wider truer real only in relation to it to re-complete it.
There is a generative logic. In re-reading it in a sense of its
long completion one comes to re-complete it in an accounting for one's self in a wider truer move now toward the real.
A more definitive statement of it. That is one's stance. Argument. Toward the true real. Now. Now the actual of this
stance come against the historical to rupture its completed
sense of the real. Its definitive statement of it. In an act of
rewriting. In a taking up and turning as an act of re-circum-
scribing. The wider true of this stance circumscribing correcting extending a definitive statement-style of the real. In
descent to novel form-style. The new true real. A voice not
yet once heard for the world. A voice which must be heard
for its own self regard. Recognized life. But it is hard to
be heard. There is the whole of history to silence one. But
within such historical severity paradoxically to be found the
dynamics of all stylistic transformation. The undoing of its
own sense of completion found residing in its great works.
In its solidity it stands to be transformed. The history of influence the logic of transformation. Discrimination. Fine
grained history of aesthetic richness. No history of style
without influence. No significant meaningful stylization of

the real as new without aesthetics of influence. The history of a literature contingently not about taste but about troping. In works and between works. Replication and rearrangement of figure. Out of a continuity of necessary turning come style generating style. It is an analytical history. It is traceable. It is normative. It is textually transformative. Intertextually bound. By necessity the constraint and extension of figured language between books books wanting to make their definitive claim. Only in relation to other books. In their relation to their epiphenomenal real the extended quality of a speaking stance ever finer in its discrimination. However wider. No stylized picture of the actual made new without complicating discriminating language in necessary relation however simple or true in diction the range the scope but only made as the new true real comparatively so held against a history of hearing a history of reading. Seeing reseen. Of writing rewriting. The real real to be figured across book-time from the persisting personality of solipsistic voice. Grounded in the phenomenal. Relevant in a history. Not any voice. No generative style but as a rhetorical stance stood in relation of the palpable self held in against a history speaking necessarily yet new of the same old real thing. Human thing. We must account for what is now worth reading and writing. There are reasons for a literature's worth. We must account for significance in a supreme narrative so. For the self. Its secular sacredness. Mortal form. Taste cannot be accounted for so. That is the critical problem. We do not want the ideology of a convention. A supreme art must be accountable. There is authentic generative ground. A normative movement toward transformation which has humanly moral reverberations. Though not about a morality. Its normativity is analytical. Its normativity the true real of mortal actuality. Supreme language as style-form a narrative extending a picture of a real significantly oriented in relation to the history of a human picture. It is an art of us. It is not an act of unconsidered expression. However abstract. It rewrites the actual as it has been said to have been seen lived in a look in a walk in grand or simple scope in a sentence in a book toward a human good. However the horror the degradation of it. The liberation of it. Toward the true of it. A newer truer constrained extension made meaningful in relation to an other way of seeing and saying the human. Disclosing it. A new word in history. To show ourselves for good. Another-way-of speaking the real. Of widening the real in the delimiting of a style. This movement in style as a generative power in correcting extending an expanding expressive language toward the disclosure of our mortal predicament. Its full situated frame. Deep style. Focus. Style a generative language-act come into being intelligibly and authoritatively upon the page out of an orienting aesthetics of influence toward the possible expression of the human. The forms of the possibly human. Of perception itself. A novel epistemology. A kind of truer science of expression. Humanity. For the good of character. A knowing held at last to be true in its tone and color for the real real. Of us ourselves in the truest story of ourselves. A generation of definitive necessary completing style-form extant and traceable over a literature in expansion in its kind and quality of supreme speaking. Deep knowing. Literature stylized in the wandering length of its continuity under stretches of its apparent discontinuity giving up its expressive width. That trajectory for the true. Literature extant as a way of reforming speaking founded in accruing accumulating widening claims for the real. The human picture rewritten reformed reseen recurrent in a stylistic act of widening significance under a logic of influence. That literary act of mortally situated invention accounting for the generation of style under the aesthetics of influence. For the self. There is that historical algorithm of refiguring the real. In books. Between books. We read it. We hear it. We see the aestheticized real in such a way in such a style in an extending expanding truer circumscribing literature in form. Toward the true. To the limits of expression. Though you cannot get to it a last word. Get the last word. No last word for the world. Or us in it. No matter the sheer sense of stylistic completion in great works. Those supreme fictions sublimely enclosing all. The perpetual stylization of the real an un-fossilized unfixed written existing thing continually reforming in relation to a history of literature in declaring defining refining stances come across the actual from book to book in the comparative relation and duration of a livid literature in its strongest amplifying books. Of vital value. To see the real of one in relation to the other. To see the difference in similarity. The agreement in disagreement. To follow out the correcting widening extension toward a true as though to a limit text by text as in a science. To a knowing of a new frontier. That kind of traceable and so capable history. The aesthetics of influence a history of style allowing authentic generation of novel readable work however experimental extended corrective antithetical. Rich. Expansive. Even if antithetical. When. To all before. But read in relation to all before. The avant-garde. Normative reaction and extension. Toward the new. The never before seen. The not yet once heard in such a way. An exploration for the ear and eye. Discovery of a new world. Metamorphic. Manifestic. Toward the as yet. Toward the as yet not expressed. Inexpressible. Nevertheless expressed. Intelligible in form reformed. Adaptable. Abstractable. The circumscription of a truer real moved toward disclosing at last the unseen the unheard. That. All unformed. But once disclosed recognizable. Or not of an art. Epiphenomenal transcendence. Art of the phenomenal. Perception sublimely rearranged. Supreme pages of it. All now seen and heard. As never before. But not apparent until so formed. An extending if not circumscribing work come round all history. Yet history allowing the work as it is. Almost an extra-historical work. In its greatness. Seeming original. Prior. Immanent in its ontology. Its form come at last to enclose in round all before it. In itself. Itself appearing to restylize history. Subsume. All that which has allowed it is at last retransformed from influence to experience. It is alchemic. It is not of the occult. However shamanistic. It is fundamental in ontic aesthetic. All encompassing like a natural law. Elemental in its prosody. Metaphysical in epistemology of epiphenomenal form. Eclipsing-enclosing adamantively all known form. A hard felt sense of literary completion for the form. The final circumscription of the world. At last the true real word for the world. The finalized final frontier limit of expression in that form. Nothing after. The one true real. There is now nothing truer. Till later.

BOOK THREE

IT MUST GIVE PLEASURE

ON THE SCENE
OF DRAMATIC INTEREST

LIVED PICTURE of VITAL IMPRESSION or MAKING the WANTING-to-KNOW. *The only obligation to which in advance we may hold a novel, without incurring the accusation of being arbitrary, is that it be interesting. That general responsibility rests upon it, but it is the only one I can think of. The ways in which it is at liberty to accomplish this result (of interesting us) strike me as innumerable, and such as can only suffer from being marked out or fenced in by prescription...A novel is in its broadest definition a personal, a direct impression of life: that, to begin with, constitutes its value, which is greater or less according to the intensity of the impression...Here it is especially that [the writer] works, step by step, like his brother of the brush, of whom we may always say that he has painted his picture in a manner best known to himself...The painter is able to teach the rudiments of his practice, and it is possible, from the study of good work (granted the aptitude), both to learn how to paint and to learn how to write...I remember an English novelist, a woman of genius, telling me that she was much commended for the impression she had managed to give in one of her tales of the nature and way of life of the French Protestant youth. She had been asked where she learned so much about this recondite being, she had been congratulated on her peculiar opportunities. These opportunities consisted in her having once, in Paris, as she ascended a staircase, passed an open door where, in the household of a pasteur, some of the young Protestants were seated at table round a finished meal. The glimpse made a picture; it lasted only a moment, but that moment was experience. She had got her direct personal impression, and she turned out her type. She knew what youth was and what Protestantism; she also had the advantage of having seen what it was to be French, so that she converted these ideas into a concrete image and produced a reality. Above all, however, she was blessed with the faculty which when you give it an inch takes an ell, and which for the artist is a much greater source of strength than any incident of residence or of place in the social scale. The power to guess the unseen from the seen, to trace the implication of things, to judge the whole piece by the pattern, the condition of feeling life in general so completely that you are well on your way to knowing any particular corner of it...If experience consist of impressions, it may be said that impressions are experience...and I may therefore venture to say that the air of reality (solidity of specification) seems to me to be the supreme virtue of a novel—the merit on which all its other merits (including that conscious moral purpose of which Mr. Besant speaks) helplessly and submissively depend. If it be not there they are all as nothing, and if these be there, they owe their effects to the success with which the author had produced the illusion of life...There are bad novels and good novels, as there are bad pictures and good pictures...I do not pretend to estimate the degree of interest proceeding from them, for this will depend upon the skill of the painter...the only classification of the novel that I can understand is into that which has life and that which has it not—James, The Art of Fiction.* A principle of interest underlies all supreme narrative. A principle of interest underlies the act of all reading. We read. We keep reading. We are interested. We see a life unfolding. We come in at a middle. Time pictured in a place. Perception. Impression. Of a life being lived. Now we want to know an end. We feel we are promised some thing. We are implicated. We must know. There is the how and the why. The lived picture implicates us. We are curious of ends and means. We imagine all things what they are could be have been when seen to be lived. People places things. When they are placed in the epiphenomenal world of a supreme fiction they accrue significance. We want to know what they are in a world. That world. Their world. The significance of objects. Made image. The arrangement of time and space. Composition of. Reverberating with the impression of life. Lives. Relations. A story emerges. A story in a style. A character. In a story in a style.

Character come in the closed focused distance. In the held duration. The dramatic scene of character formed in the axis of distance-duration. To hold the human. To hold the human close. Pages of perception. Unfolding. A point of view is a self at stake. A narrative. Or say nothing. Language comes of it. Style. Story-style. We want to know what is at stake. All is at stake. Dramatic interest come of mortal action. However ordinary. Nothing is ordinary. The simplest action extraordinary in the epiphenomenal actual. The possibility of the world contained in the lifting of a hand. A look. All is of implication. In the stakes of another. Of the eye the ear focused on the life of invested action. Enacted. Not action per se but pictured action of a necessary real. Enactment of interest driven in necessity. That extant ongoing real born to the page in that language. That language disclosing its dramatic interest in the real of an already extant world. Teeming in necessity. A world we want to access in its passing so. In the vibrant disclosure. Enter. To live in. Awhile. As in a life. Voyeuristically inhabit. But vitally. The dramatic interest of scene the focus of the extant necessity of what is at stake. At that spot. Held so. Framed so. All such paintings of supreme narrative impression as art come to the page have a frame and focus. All painting has a frame and focus. Or not an art. So many heard words on a page making a picture of this size and shape that color and depth of view in a light this perspective that distance to persons and things. Tone-color focused in stylizing an action in the dramatic quality of its sounded out act. There is a central logic of focus to a dramatic language. Delineation of the real. It is built. It is got to. We must get to it. A felt picture in passing making a want to know revealing an unseen story in the arrangement of its objects made image in focus. Relevance. To that world. In that held spot in passing necessary time. Composition of feeling. Thinking. Judging. Acting. Being. Dramatic interest begun in the eye. The ear. In the dynamic perception of passing. The epiphenomenal from the phenomenal. A supreme narrative a durational however elliptical gallery of picture forming subject. Interest of specific selves mortally generalized. Lividly recognizable. Narrative animates. One picture placed so against another animates. An affective logic of the life forms. Character constrained in passing enactment livid in an already extant world making our wanting to know in a narrative a heard picture of mortally necessary selected seen things put one up against the other so to form an affective logic. All livid significant sights of story as focused phenomenality in object reseen into image so in the making of a supreme epiphenomenal impression. Mise-en-scene. Setting is somatic perception in transcendence. Character psychic state. All in a sequence of vital impression enacted in passing a formal principle of dramatic interest. However elliptical in continuity. For perception never cut. No cutting of the perceived. All non-linearity of act action object image must be perceived. Or no art in continuity or not. Dramatic sequence the juxtaposition of perception. A congregation of objects

and selves transcending their surfaces to image and character. Impinging upon the perceptive life. Of the reader. Mortal
life. Implicating. Mimetic material made diegetically significant in implication. In narrative. In reading. Symbol-led. In
time. In telling time. Perception gone into the symbolic in
time. Interest anchored in the passing necessary significant
real of cause and consequence. That real for the dramatic.
That dramatic real. In the temporal distance between the now
and the possibly to be. Interest. Between the what was and
the now to be. Dramatic implication in interpretation. Of
cause and consequence. In the distance of being and remembering. Projecting and being. That discontinuity. Ellipticality. Replete in the continuity of perception. Richness. Vivid-
ness of a life unfettered constrained. Remembering feeling
and projecting possibility the dramatic interest of what is at
stake now for the self arriving to the page in the formation of
necessary action enacted in a language on a page in a life
lived and held right there now in its own time. Focus. There
is a felt and seen world living before us in terms of itself. It
is ongoing and prior to our knowing of it in its real. We
come to it. We want to know what will come of it good or
bad. We read on out of the middle of it. Narrative arrangement a somatic-psychic order of picture compelling us to
want to know of a world of another's worldly want of some
good no matter if good or not. Our interest to know formed
in the sensation of picture. In time. Arrangement and congregation of placed repeated object and action a sequence con-

straining a want into recurrent image to significance. The sensation of picture turned to a mortal subject of what one wants. In necessity. In time. Vital impression the aesthetic strength of the somatic eye. All person and placed thing action character consequence comprised of a visual analytic. Style the personality of picture. Heraclitus says character is destiny. In a supreme narrative character is picture. The subject-self framed constrained. Dramatic interest arriving most strictly out of a pictured subject-self seen so. Whatever narrative comment come of all what is seen so. But picture first. Or no authentic judgment-comment however true. We must have a world within which to judge. There is the real. One must have one's real to talk of. Character. Character-picture. No character without a closing psychic distance. Focus. This animation of the self into the subject. Action. The panoramic world become individualized in the distance of language. The focus of a lens of language gone from mountain and sky to face and eye. One closes that mimetic distance in picture to know the character as individual subject. Diegetic in telling. Or all is inanimate. All surface. Impenetrable sheerness. All simply light and rock and we want to know that light this rock against that face and eye. That face and this eye means. So it means. So something is at stake. So our interest to know what all will happen in a life. This interest to know and our feeling that wanting a dramatic interest wanting to subsume and to contain all other narrative interests. We simply must know. In time. There is an atavistic curiosity. It is us. What will happen? In a life. We hold it to our life. The life informs the dramatic relevance of the work. That circumscribing interest a self interest. Narrative dramatic only because of this life. The true drama has always been the life. The dramatic interest to know how a place in a time is lived. To see it pictured. To go through it the good the bad. To feel the lived life. A kind of moral want of life. To be implicated so. To go through so. The only way out is through. To go again through. So in a world. One may live in another's well awhile. That pleasure awhile. Rejuvenation in the dramatic correspondence of lives. Recognition of life. Of its secular sacredness and sense. Dramatic unrepeatability. The want to repeat. To hold the life in duration. A mortal made moral want in a narrative in a reader in a character come out of aestheticized picture closed in distance and held in duration. Some good must surely come of the dramatic self in time. We think so for others. If not surely for ourselves. We wait and see. We must wait. We see. We feel. We are shown what it is a life what is at stake in a look or in a hand. There are these looks and those hands. Picture implicates. In action. In time. In cause and consequence. From at least the time of the Greeks the dramatic picturing of the individual as a mortal-moral subject. Character. The ancient novel closes the psychic distance of the epic. The pictoral presentation of the individual appears. We are in the world of the living individual in Achilles Tatius's *Kleitophon and Leukippe*. Genre itself is a closing or opening of psychic distance. For dramatic char-

acter. Interest in the correspondence of art to livid life. A supreme fiction pictoral-time closed upon the individual. We
know who is speaking or spoken about. As an epiphenomenal individual. We want to know what has or will happen to
them. Out of picture impression made character this dramatic
interest to know arriving structurally durationally out of
what is held to be at stake for another in a seen felt place pictured over time. The dramatic as an interest is a formal struc-
tural logic of the scenic subject seen. Heard. Held. Phenomenal on the epiphenomenal page. Even in Beckett. There is
the world of the sensible individual. Then there is talk turned
on picture. Perception itself made moral in mortal sentiment.
However elliptical in continuity. In character. But no true
talk without pictured thing person or place. Dramatized aestheticized intellectualized real of stone and stick and hand
and room. Not the reportage of historical events or tenets of
a philosophy conceptual and intellectual exploration of an
idea without the phenomenal albeit it contain those acts of
ranging ruminating knowing within the pictoral impression-
interest of its dramatic drive in a world. The epiphenomenal
mind may proliferate in the phenomenal impression of a pictured world. The mind is its own place but only in a world.
In a place. A phenomenal context of intellection. A scene of
sense. No matter how innovative or experimental the form of
the fiction first we are interested in it implicated in it and
most fundamentally in terms of its picturing an extant real.
However fable-istic fantastic or surreal in form and language

yet pictured placed. Yet the anchor of the eye for the ear to know a world where something is at stake. Then there is the dramatic. We can read Kafka and Beckett. We can see ourselves. We see new things in our old selves. We can read Kafka and Beckett and we feel ourselves. Those rooms those things are our rooms and things. They are pictured familiar and real in a world however strange. The world is strange. Extraordinary. The actual supreme art never ordinary. Not life. Such things striking however never too unfamiliar. Not too estranged to be unrecognizable. They contain emotional residue. Feeling for life. Life is striking. Extraordinary. Their rooms as rooms contain the more than the residue of life lived for the somatic eye. A point of view in striking perception. Picture. Story. Style. Significance in such seen things. But again one must close upon picture. One must focus and forge a picture. Tone of impression. Dramatic texture pictured in time. Picture in duration extends and contracts narrative. Makes formal patterned discriminations of light and dark. The tone-tenor of perception. Makes the actual significant in terms of the self at stake. But if nothing. Picture must close and hold upon a personality in time. Personality perceived in pages of perception. Present on a page. All the dramatic lives in the personality in constraint. In question. In doubt. In possibility. In duration. In decision. Spots of consciousness made into consequence. A look a turn of the head held in all its significance and constraint in a world held in a scenic logic of the real. A mortal pictoral time of perception.

Intellection. Emotion. Impression. The dramatic interest the Greeks knew of long ago and formed in picture. In action. We are not at all different. We persist in the same aesthetic. Perception persists beyond convention. The analytic is beyond taste. This pictoral drive of dramatic interest. Loss pictured. Regret structured. The emotive scenic. The affective analytical. Wanting and losing algorithmic. Tell me we are otherwise. We are not. We are yet no one of us no different. To feel the felt life. An analytic of the feeling pictured. The moral pictured. There there is dramatic interest impressed. A dramatic good a visual dialectic. In picture first. Action. Of consequence. So to feel the felt life present before one of another so to be implicated. The dramatic grounded in a logic of the scenic. The human held. Present to be unfolded. The true drama has always been the enacted life. Its consequence. The soundings out of a life. The life as it is lived. To be lived so. Vital impression. An art that does not pass over to simply what is next. That correspondence of lived life in an art. The Greek. The Shakespearian stage. That dramatic scene in act. That mimetics infused with diegetics. Extended in a supreme fiction. Vision. Implication. A dramatic interest of pictured stakes for the self holding the human before us to become a mortal interest. In supreme narrative the wanting-to-know become a moral want made of picture. To see what possible good may come in time to character perceived on a page. That stage for all the world. To turn the page. To know. To know that good.

ON THE SENSE
OF AESTHETIC INTEREST

SENSIBILITY of LANGUAGE or the INTELLIGIBLE MUSIC of a NARRATIVE SELF. *They were rooms of that country order which—just as in certain climes whole tracts of air or ocean are illuminated or scented by myriads of protozoa which we cannot see—enchants us with the countless odours emanating from the virtues, wisdom, habits, a whole secret system of life, invisible, superabundant and profoundly moral, which their atmosphere holds in solution; smells natural enough indeed, and weather-tinted like those of the neighbouring countryside, but already humanized, domesticated, snug, an exquisite, limpid jelly skillfully blended from all the fruits of the year which have left the orchard for the storeroom, smells changing with the season, but plenishing and homely, offsetting the sharpness of hoarfrost with the sweetness of warm bread, smells lazy and punctual as a village clock, roving and settled, heedless and provident, linen smells, morning smells, pious smells, rejoicing in a peace which brings only additional anxiety, and in a prosaicness which serves as a deep reservoir of poetry to the stranger who passes through their midst without having lived among them—Proust, In Search of Lost Time.* All narrations of any supremacy are inflected in rich acts of sense and sensation. Of an internal elegance of proportion and order. Of a whole in terms of themselves as parts. The range of perception on the page the capability of the nature of the quality and kinds of the epiphenomenal view actualized in a language arranged out of the nature of a perceiving personality. Into an art. A narration of consequence is a perception of some personality. Narrator character. A view with a voice. A how with a who. Narrative order and proportion here come into being in their aptness and animation as an induction of a personality of some perception. Personality as an ordering quality become a rhetorical instrument for exploring the aesthetic possibilities of a fictive language. The expressive limits of a language and its kinds of figures formed in the actuality of an art of some necessity. Narrative an aesthetic project of intellection sensed sensibility in a singular dynamic prosody bearing all the apt real. Not static. Dynamic. Progressive. Integrative. Vital. Internally rational to its wildest expressivity. Whole in its risk to discover. Perception a prosody. Language of aesthetic interest that is a claim for the rich real and its reverberations. The world is spoken. What is said is seen. Picture. Troped. A picture demands a prosody. A prosody a question of aesthetic interest. A story prosody. A style story. One might say that language is what was and will be new

under the sun. No matter the same old world. Story. One
would not be wrong. Narrative as knowing even as a prosodic art-science speaks of the same world. The world has not
changed. Arrangement changes. Composition alters. Prosody
digs deeper into story. World. Aesthetics a palpable instrument of discovery exploration investigation. A Meta-Sense.
To perceive all the phenomenal and epiphenomenal. The
world again new and unexpected. In supreme narrative. Prosodic art-science. Widens the true to get to the real. Shake-
speare knew that. How to put the world on a stage. Newton
knew that in natural philosophy. How to put all the world
on a page. Beneath prosody all old plots become supreme.
Sublime. All effects re-affected. The natural sublime has always been rationally confounding to the perception of pan-
orama to the ontic eye to the predictive motion of celestial
bodies. So it is as a prosody confounding to the sheer causality of plot. To overcome the sheerness of plot. A source
of speaking feeling to the causal act. To irony. To tragedy.
No matter same cause of event. Effect. Productive of feeling of a language of feeling of emotive transport in the very
intellection of its proportion and order as integrated form toward lividness and exploration of life in its arrangement as
a whole. There are happily the great elusive things language
yet pursues in sound and sense. To enrichen cause. There is
that making sense and sensation reformed in an as yet novel
composition of language in new arrangement in the sounding
of a thing. As in the composition of symphonic orchestration

from a constrained scale key harmonics in a novel arrangement of notation made vital music. It is emotive. We are interested in sense as sound. Interested in the sound of sense as a somatic thing. Aesthetic interest the somatic pleasure of a prosody. This pleasure a rooted sense. This pleasure the atavistic sense of a somatics sounding out in the sentence. In the ear. The sentence a felt thing. A dramatic compression of the phenomenal in prosody. There is dramatic interest in a prosody as in a heard sound seen picture. Syntactical rhythm of vision. The language of the sentence as sound and sense figure-trope with which to see and to see so in such a way a picture compressing a story in a style. The very use of language in itself embedding the very dramatic interest of story compressing an emotional narrative presentation of the dramatic into the very use of language. In this compression dialectically connecting what is held to be at stake in a story for a self to the particular expression of a sentence. The weighted inflected ranging perception of narrator or character or narrator as character infusing a particular expression compression to the prose. Perception on a page. Building the interior of all picture in prosody. All person place thing. Prosody the vital interior of scenic picture. Of whatever compression-extension. The palpability of object made image the quality of language. Register. Tone. Tenor. Discrimination. Intellection. Circulation. Recurrence. An object made to image of specific quality in a closing or opening of distance in a duration a function of a schematic prosody.

Dramatic lyrical interest necessarily compressed in the art of the prose in a particular way of speaking the story to significance. A speaking significance which makes that story speak in a way another would not. Cannot. A language as an aesthetic interest employing a particular selection range register of diction high or low or narrow or wide the sentence going on forward to negotiate between such levels of feeling as sound and sense carrying a story so in a particular prosody over the texture of a narrative. A narrative as a story textured so and in that way. Singular. Definitive. A story demands a prosody. A picture demands a prosody. Or we cannot see its quality of stance as the utterance toward story as stake the argument of the drama of the self of the speaking of such a mortal vision made art out of a way of seeing feeling. All this the sense of a sound sounding out the quality of a scenic picture the scenic picture made of a perception so to be seen so to be felt so. So to be held in its real. Prosody what is seen and felt sounded and heard so of a stance at stake in its real. One which must be sounded in such word to be heard in its real. To be seen. The necessary work of words. This phenomenal set of dialectical elements to a style. Seen and sounded word sentence figure of speech become figure of exploration to discover the new and unexpected in the dynamic integration of troped parts fused on a page in a kind of singing of the soul at stake animated in its necessity of singular expression. Part troped to dynamic whole in felt talk of the world at stake. In arrangement. Composition. Singularly sung. Heard. Apt aesthetics a somatics. Actuality of style. No matter that that style as a stance be a thing written against a history of style. Differentiating itself in its specific quality of similar element. For in the interior of such a style there is a style of the actual. Different in arrangement. Yet atavistic in its phenomenality. Leading to all epiphenomenality. Arrangement. The analytical somatic element of style. To see. To feel. To hear. To taste. To smell. The Proustian trope of smell none of it of a taste. This atavistics of element none of it as a sense ever a style put against or received of a history under an aesthetics of influence. No matter that that influence come all cross it. Rather first this real sense of sensation as the very ability of a style. The somatic atavistic root of a style to be. Of a perception and its prosodic capabilities in action in time. Possibilities of artistic kind. A style a prosody of aesthetic interest the induction of sense itself as a source no matter a style's historical deduction as a correction extending of a prior style once inducted into an arrangement. There in such sense as a source there is presentation of sounding syntactical rhythm under feeling thinking. The very feltness of word. Thought. The old drive of syntax a somatic sense. The persisting palpability of the sentence. The emotion of the paragraph. The high register of a repetition a felt attitude of some flight. A flight or a longing come to a page as in an actual fear. The work of words. The very attitude of accrual. Hunting gathering. Recollecting. Listing. Amplifying. All provisions in a prosody. A heard dynamics dramatics of the mortal such figures. That sense inducted to style. No style without this ground. No picture put in focus. No apt drawing of the dramatic. The self. Happily we may hear what to draw. To see. No matter it come most strongly to us only in time. In time it comes. Vividly. Clearly. There is a rhetoric of temporal distance to a supreme language. There is an act of recollection to finding a prosody. A temporal distance opened to be closed from narrative thing to word. Thing then to word now. Object to image. Object of one time to image of another. Toward significance in things places people told now of in another time. Language comes of it. Aesthetic interest. Language drawn as in a rich source from the opening prosody as it closes now in upon recollected picture. Remembering feeling. Refiguring the real. Feeling that hearing word by word to seeing feeling on the page in a prosody. Language not ever the opposite of picture itself. All what makes the dimension of picture. The quality of picture. Feeling. Perception. It is a rudimentary aesthetics. Of all interest. That sourced language driven from the heard and felt as a mortal music making picture. The sound of a primal scene. Remembering feeling. Emotive syntax visual extension. The interior substance of all surface sensed. The soul in the eye. Ear. Voice. All now to be told of the actual. Once nothing to be told of it. Prosody not found for it. No aesthetic interest in a life. But in time. In time all told of it. Now all to come. Now it is actual as remembrance. Now the object an image of residue. Now the aesthetic word exceeds the surface of the object. Now one can make it real as it was. More than real. Make it mean. Epiphenomenally. Aesthetically. In the telling time of narrative arrangement. One knows nothing in sheer naming. Everything in narrative. One knows nothing but in narrative. In distance. Telling. The interest of the world is the aestheticized world. Now significance forms about it. Language the structure of remembrance. Aesthetic interest a style of sense a rhetoric of sensation moving driving as a distant closing recurrence of a language toward the recovery of a palpable real. Time cannot be lost. Supreme narrative the recovery of a palpable real as it is. As it was. As it is in meaning. A temporal distance a generative act of aesthetic capability in supreme narrative. Generating aesthetic interest. Come as an ellipsis of time there on a page opening a language to a source of speaking in the gap between the vision of a person a place a thing in a diegetic now held against its being recollected in a past real. The difference in the time of the telling of the act and the time of the act. To deliver in recollection all the residue of a life in its significance to a page. In remembering feeling. This rearrangement of the real. It is an essential opening up of language. This closing of the distance in aestheticized word between past object made present image. A source of a quality of language as a visual kind to color a picture to symbolize sensation. Therein a supreme dimension of picture. Fullness of clarity. It is an emotive dimension. A wholeness in integrity of form. The ranging proportion and integrity of the clarity of knowing a life in time in things. In the recurrence of a language made more of significance than of things. Chairs put in rooms and sat in so are sat in in-such-a-way. There is a look which contains all other looks. A love that contains all loves. A smell a touch. The containment of all other smell and touch. All in such a prosody affectively focused. Superimposed. The once seen reseen. Once felt refelt. More than furniture moving in scenic structure. The diegetic life of summary cast in substance. More than the what-happens-next. Setting here ever symbolic. Picture deep perception more than sight. Mortally felt more than ever seen. Diegetics subsuming mimetics. Essential telling inside all showing. Picture acutely heard. Emotic sense emerging through the surface of the seen. Transcendence of the material to the spiritual. The phenomenal to the epiphenomenal. Aesthetic interest in all such transcendence. Then in the syntax acoustics a rhythm wrapped in a rhetoric an argument for richness of form fullness of self come on in sense and sensation. Sense come to take a sounding stance. All sensation on the page sound and speed full of argument. Tone driven. Pace a deduction. An argued attitude. Alliteration. Leading by ear sounding out an argument. The words fall by tenor in logical place. We hear the authority of the argument. It sounds right. The intelligible music of a narrative. This is the way the world is for this voice and no other. It is felt so. It is said so. It is seen so. This world sounds and is so. The work becomes what it is. Is as a whole as it is. Has proportion and integrity. Completes itself. Has fullness of form. Is vital in the dynamic coordination of its own parts. Is aesthetically expressed actuality as art. Significant. The Thomistic aesthetic. A progressive integration of elements made dynamic. Of affecting aesthetic interest. Able to be known in its fullness and richness of form in the clarity of the implicated eye of the reader's looking. Reading. The reader reads on. Story takes shape in a prosody. Ever hidden in language. The revelation made in increments. In the foraging of sentences searching for story. The old rhythm of going forward to find. The root of syntax. The elevation of register. One must go. Get on. All to come is new. There is the promise of finding. There is pleasure in the promise of finding. There is surprise. There is pleasure in surprise. The promise itself is an interest. A language presents and works up a new world in working words. A stance a way of speaking makes a new logic a new sentence a grammar we follow in a promise of finding however hard to follow. The promise of this new language this new world a leading language. A sounding leading a logic an ellipsis a new grammar run to sense in the promise of finding. The feeling of it. Sound driving a sentence forward hard as a logic as a grammar taken up carried on we are keeping up to follow on to where we do not know where in such promise almost more by ear than intellect all going on away into the compositional terrain of new narrative time and space in the as yet unknown arrangement of the proportion of the form ordering itself into a whole. Which knows

itself. Which has integrity and proportion to its knowing itself in a fullness which we follow. Which we are following
on into after livid living sentences. The promise of the pleasure of the following the sounding persistence of new and
unexpected fullness in the sentence before all but bearing the
real of the story in each such sounding. It must be more than
page turning. One should want to read a book again. There
is the sense of all to come again and again in a supreme narrative. It is in its aesthetic promise of the vital and the true.
The perpetual reliving of that. A world made. An ontological journey. Yet a book in hand. All true real world made
corporeal to a consciousness. A prosody coordinating all the
elemental working parts of the dynamic integrity of the integrated and progressive form. On a page made first of words.
Phrases. Sentences. Paragraphs. Scenes. Summaries. Chap-
ters. Books. In a variety of kinds and lengths across textual
space. This elemental demarcation of text on a page all so
many conventional parts unified in their Story-Order and
Style-Proportion in accordance to the aesthetics of the art as
a composition an arrangement of textual space in an integrated elegance aptness of what is at stake in a view a voice. On
a page made then of figures of speech of the troping of textual space. The convention turned. Made full of form. To complete its form. All fitted to form. Informed. Of simile. Metaphor. Metonymy. Analepsis. Prolepsis. The ability of the
mind's ranging perception. Remembrance and projection. In
time. Anachrony. Synchrony. Syllepsis. Praxis. Peripeteia of

praxis. With Paralipsis. Then paralepsis. The whole dramatic endurance of character in action. Of how to tell. Of when
to tell. Of what to tell when. To who. Of whom. Of character. Story made so in filled out form of aesthetic interest. Of
anisochrony. Narrative speed. Of movement from scene to
summary. Of catalysis in summary. Then of deictic contex-
tualization to place time and person for subsequent scene. To
anchor the actual. Orient the real of now. The dialectic of en-
chainment for transformation of character in continuity. Or
the isochrony of duration for a constant speed of unfolding
event in time. A montage of motifs. Leitmotifs of isotopy.
All this figured on a page made first of words to inform the
integrity and proportion of the composition the coordination
of the arrangement of parts to whole in the fullness of form.
In the endless combination and recombination of their figures to form the new and unexpected in an infinity of wholes
in an unlimited number of integrities and proportions in the
actuality of an art. A lineage of the Thomistic aesthetic. In
dynamics of pattern of texture of tension in the animated integration of figures materially forged fused in their exploration one within the other in the integrity and proportion of a
kind of singing of the soul at stake. A supreme fiction a progressive integrated whole full necessary dynamic animated
actual new explorative unexpected compulsory inexhaustible
art.

ON THE PLEASURE
OF INTELLECTUAL INTEREST

AESTHETICIZING IDEA or SERIOUS PHILOSOPHICAL PLAY. *He may likewise consider, how differently he is affected by the same Thought, which presents it self in a great Writer, from what he is when he finds it delivered by a Person of an ordinary Genius. For there is as much difference in apprehending a Thought cloathed in Cicero's Language, and that of a common Author, as in seeing an Object by the Light of a Taper, or by the Light of the Sun—Addison, Spectator No. 409.* There are novels of ideas. There are narratives containing intellectual history. There are narratives playing with intellectual history. It is one of the pleasures of reading. Such playing with sense as a conceptual space. Not the somatic-emotive per se. Yet no idea but in the sensed thing. The act. Even in Beckett. Intellectual interest as a mental pleasure is aestheticized in a supreme narrative in direct relation to persons places and things. The possibility of an intellectual good pursued is pursued rhetorically in figure. Figured in its apt expression on a page in relation to the narrative art as a whole. Its subject may be of a moral interest. It is all dialectical. Yet the possibility of an idea. The possibility of an idea in the first place is the possibility of a language. The possibility of a language is the possibility of an aesthetic. It is analytical. It is serious rigorous play. The depth and breadth of a consciousness in duration. Of a perception on a page. It is not for the weak. It requires work. It is a sounding out of the mind. It is the holding of a supreme narrative in its place and letting it dig down to what all may be found in following the logic of a sound. In thinking. Recollecting the self. The logic of a sound and the anchor of a time and a place in a text in a sentence must aestheticize in some expressive substance and proportion of form an authentic idea of essence to a self in a narrative of any supremacy. An authentic intellection cannot exceed the art. It embodies the whole of the order of the form. While enriching it. An authentic idea pursued in the thought of a self contains the authority of a voice surrounded by a room or a look. A voice constrained. A voice constrained pursues a concept. A self. A concept a self cannot stand alone in significance without a voice constrained. It is naked. It is bare. It is philosophy. Not self. It is empty of dramatic scenic somatic psychic relevance no matter if supremely true. It may only stand so as true to such an introspecting self within the palpability of a voice which believes in the aptness and the wisdom of the idea or thought pursued as a narrative texture. It may take form in a sentence as a kind of claim for the true. It may take form in a sentence as a kind of sum of the real. It may take form in a sentence as a kind of normative judgment cast across all to take up the true real once and for all in one spot in one sentence no matter the extending duration of its impression. It is a compressing and a widening the claim and the sum as kinds of language. Such declarations must be earned. Must be anchored. Must be scenically purchased. Grounded. Introspection must be prospected. Are sourced from inside the work as a whole. Not laid upon it. All aside come from the inside. Then interiority of such claiming thought may fall upon an act or a consequence upon a person as the voice of a god. When it falls in the right good place. It must fall there or bear no reality to the page. Come as a kind of crystallization claimed there in its integrity of stopped spot. Narrative time on hold for the sum or claim. The scene has stopped for the judging mind to speak. It is a kind of aside. Narrative supremely extended in a kind of soliloquy. A space of opening in the narrative. The speaking one's mind. The very extension of a mind. A voice wrapping its thinking round the world in a language. A claim circumscribing all that has come. Preparing for what may come. Hamlet or Beckett. The form no different in its circumscribing intellect. Claiming to know the true for that time and place as a god knows. Even if in doubt. Most truly godlike of self-begotten self when in doubt. It will be lyrical no matter its idea. It will be elegiac no matter its normativity. It is somatic language despite its conceptuality. It is the compression of conceptuality into regret or longing into mortal affect such intellection. Philosophizing feeling. Earned philosophizing. The lament of the idea. A mortal normative ethics such language. The narrating voice become almost a moral guide when believing so in itself in that place in that sentence stopping the story so and in such a way believed in so because of placed sentence in form. Palpable sentence. Introspection sensation. The time of the narrative stopped and held dug into even as it is to be extended in an idea-thought made material made aptly manifest in a syntax in a diction in a rhythm in a register of accumulation accretion repetition its scope its depth its width of conceptual space made authentic present corporeal on a page no matter it all be the plumbing of a consciousness. The plumbing of a perception of acute intellect one of the most corporeal acts of the somatic self. In a somatic aestheticized ethics the intellectual plumbing heard and felt as consequential reverberation of self as no philosophical idea can be stood alone. The livid intellect. The idea married to the language. To the stake of the self in question. Feeling thinking. Doubting hoping. It cannot be otherwise. It is not. The aestheticized sentence sounding leading the logic as a heard thing of ideational sense organically necessarily transcended. Feeling-thinking. Phenomenal-epiphenomenal. Actual-art. The phenomenal persisting acutely intellected in the epiphenomenal. Sensation-sense. A music of the actual. The sense of the mortal. Yet a kind of play. The extension of the intellected idea the proliferating word now come into be-

ing on the page as a musical motif to be heard in all its discriminating variations. Distinctions. Proliferations. Making
its own time. Improvisation grounded in feeling out the
sound of an idea pursued. Thought. It begins its own duration. Makes its own durational real in the aestheticized time
of the idea-motif. A complicating harmonics. Intellect pictured. On a page. There is time and time to think in narrative.
One may take one's time. Exhaust one's thoughts. But one
must hear them. One must follow out the sound of them.
Their sense comes in the sensation of them. One must cast
them in expression in dynamic proportion to the whole as an
essential integral figured part of a compositional art. Of an
actuality. Integrity of magnitude on the page. One must put
them against rooms and looks and hands and wants. Put
them inside rooms and looks and hands and wants. They
must be compulsive to the real. That real. Necessary. Un-
ceaseable in their durational spot. Action turned at last to interiority as if to another story in a story. As if toward the true
story in the story in the tonality and tenor of a heard thought
sounded out made out of the time and place and persons in
correspondence of a concrete constraint. Intellection as a vital capability a narrative interest a virtuosity of play a pleasure of play held against all concrete constraint. Happily the
mind is its own place. The text opens. Consciousness cannot
be constrained. Is not in its acute necessity of perception. We
cannot forget that. We have forgot that. We must find ways
to allow that. On a page. Pages of perception. In supreme

127

narrative. A trump of taste. The opened up ranging of a language in a voice of formal integrity. Ruminating its solipsistic motifs. The intellected motif in recurrence pursued in its own durational real. Across a narrative. Spanning its whole in transformational fullness. Portioning itself out in direct relation to the dramatic or moral recurrence of its motifs as an act of aesthetic proportion. Of form. The ruminating mind unfolding in another unpassing duration in its variations held onto as an exploratory language ever ongoing in its own durational ideational real an epiphenomenal dwelling spot outside all phenomenal time of stopped scene. Hamlet. The spot as large as the ruminating consciousness. Larger than the stage. A language without limit in all its vital variations. Sublime in its confounding delimitation of scenic timespace. Covering all time and space in remembrance and projection as scene never can. Analepsis. Prolepsis. But come as epiphenomenal form from within it. Emotive in its intellect. Solipsistic introspection the fine art of the self within the drama of the self. An extra richness of the form. A necessary fullness. Intellected thoughts of the self a fullness of the form in the drama of the self. The perceptual progression of emotive sound sounding syntax syllogism of the self. Its motif at bottom mortal. Material. An intellectual interest is a mortal moral interest. In its good order an aesthetic interest. A good. The interior expansion of scene for the good of self. The exposed richness of the center of the self. Essentially expressed. Formed fully. The scene from the inside out in the bared self. Interiority diegetically told to show the unseen self. The exhaustion and extension of the known self to the self in a sequence of recurrent thought in transformation across a work. A life. All time. Place. In motif. In recurrence. In motifs turned to all possible registers and variations of their persistence. To transformational significance in an intellected aesthetic. For a self. For the whole of a work. Extending yet returning. The very pursuit of the intellected motif as the pursuit of the self. In possibility and variation. In constraint and completion. In resolution. Absolution. It is a good. Such intellection. Interiority of integrity. Variation extension discrimination the distinction of a self forming a self in the good of a rich aesthetic form. All shades of significance. Realized in figured inflected intellection. One did not know one's self so until one thought it. One did not see it. Until one heard it. One did not assume it until one said it. Character. The character of character. Residing in the richest possible real. The mind has never got to the end of a motif. A self. To the end of intellected proportion and integrity. Infinite. Expressive. New and unexpected. Every possibility yet to be explored. Combinations. Recombinations. Explorations of mortal consciousness. Revelations of the self. Pursuit of the self. Of the story. We will never write the last sentence. No last thought. Intellect sustains. The sentence cannot be exhausted. There are whole books made so.

ON THE GOOD
OF MORAL INTEREST

MORTAL PURSUIT of THE GOOD or DRAMATIC LOG-
IC. *"No, but I'll tell you one thing: I could kill and rob that
cursed old woman, and that, I assure you, without any re-
morse,"* the student added... *"I was joking just now, but look:
on the one hand you have a stupid, meaningless, worthless,
wicked, sick old crone, no good to anyone and, on the con-
trary, harmful to everyone, who doesn't know herself why
she's alive, and who will die on her own tomorrow. Understand? Understand?...A hundred, a thousand good deeds and
undertakings that could be arranged and set going by the
money that old woman has doomed to the monastery! Hundreds, maybe thousands of lives put right; dozens of families
saved from destitution, from decay, from ruin, from depravi-
ty, from the venereal hospitals—all on her money. Kill her
and take her money, so that afterwards with its help you can
devote yourself to the service of all mankind and the common cause: what do you think, wouldn't thousands of good
deeds make up for one tiny little crime? For one life, thou-*

sands of lives saved from decay and corruption. One death for hundreds of lives—it's simple arithmetic!"—Dostoevsky, Crime and Punishment. Whether of a killing done or of a loving lost or of a direness endured a supreme narrative enacts a kind of primal moral scene implicated in the logic of its dramatic interest. A moral integrity of the art pursues a mortal consequence unfolding in the dramatic. There is the coming to know this or that good in the telling as a mortal revelation so that judgments can be made. We are compelled by the good and the bad. We read for that interest on every page. However consciously. We turn pages for it. We do not exactly want to know simply what happens next. So sheerly. Thinly. Pruriently. We want to know what good or bad happens. In a rich way. An actual way. In a judging way. It is more than an idle curiosity. It is a claim for a character. We make claims for characters. As we do for ourselves. As characters make claims for themselves. Turned off mortal pictures. Sequences of actions. It is normative. Not a morality. A question of the moral. An analytical moral interest. A normative ethics of a character is constant in evaluation across a story. In evaluation in an action. In the pursuit of a good. There is an intensity of interest in the pursuit of a good. An aesthetics of interest in the dramatic the intellectual the moral all as qualities of a mortal picture in action. In a supreme narrative we are implicated morally and intellectually within the dramatic picture. The dramatic mortal wanting of a character as a possible good held in a scene. The human held.

The wanting to know is the wanting to know what good will happen. A good is held to be in question. Always in question. We make a judgment about that good. We want to know more. To gather evidence across pages. We want to know what the narrative knows. The good of a character comes in accrual. There is a great hiddeness to be revealed to a necessary good. To a generative good. To a dramatic good. To all one's language of it. We read on. We are held in the want of the good. An argued good accruing across a narrative. Amplified in action. Moral interest subsumed in the action of dramatic interest. In dramatic interest all moral interest. In a sequence of ordered proportion and integration of expressive narrative of such human essence a persisting aesthetic interest. In the good of story come the beauty of its expression. In moral interest the work of art transformed into an aesthetic interest. This transcendence. The good of the proportion the integrity of the art. It is a rich view of reading. Writing. However atavistic. Almost rudimentary in its richness. We recognize ourselves most in it. That proportion of the moral. Its manifestations. The question of it. The form of it. What is mortally at stake in a world is a question of the good within which we form ourselves. Inform. Why act and what for? How? In relation to what? One tells oneself a mortal story of the good to go do anything in a world. To do anything necessary in a narrative. A good pursued to be vitally seen in an art the dramatic interest of a passing life in question on a page. A life constrained in its living. The true drama has always been the life. The life informs the work. The life constrained in consequences of its history. History's continuing residue for the individual. For the frame of the good and the bad. Of action. The fact of an ontological history to inform the art of moral interest. A book must be written in a world. Its historical and cultural frame for the life cast as a frame of moral inquiry for the individual. Character. For aestheticized self. Supreme narrative makes a correspondence between the world and the art in the aesthetic form of moral interest. Narrative constraint of mortal consequence in an art the true real of a history come against the pursuit of a good. On a page. Constrained narrative containing the true real of a history in the actuality of its persons places things made significant to a self in a pursuit of a good on a page. Dramatic action of a story. However framed in good outcome or not. Again and again a life as a real felt to be at stake. In the actuality of a supreme art. The good is in question. In exploration. It must be as in a life. We must know what good is to come. Or not. The logic of a dramatic interest a kind of scenic structure a sequence of moral interest. Figured. Followed. Duration the continuity or ellipsis cutting or extending in focalizing scene or sum a sequence formed and ordered in its center under the arrangement of a normative ethics. Moral interest inducing form. A moral interest inducting a composition of the arrangement of the good. To be explored. That analytical structure. Whatever content. Sensed to be mortal. Not moralizing. Merely the mortal palpable pursuit of a good felt to be at stake. Perhaps already lost. The self in search of an unknown good. That pursuit of a language. The pursuit of the good for the foundered self. Of the foundered self. That interest making character in consequence. Unmaking character. We look. We see. We judge. We all judge. There is much at stake after all. Who is one? How is one? In what act does one find one's self? In what regret? In what wrong? In what right? That moral interest making character. Unmaking character. From the intellected interior. From the judged exterior. One's own and another's. Diegetic-mimetics. The character pictured. Enacted. Then judged. The claim of character turned off picture. Action. However analytical or normative or intellectual all claim to judge made off a mortal picture of a good pursued whether good or not. Whether got or not. Character-picture made and unmade in the good judged. In an art as in a life. Character-picture constrained. A constraint and a pursuit all a questioning of coalescing character. A sequence of collecting character. An implication of a self. An integrity of self. A good of dramatic logic the moral interest of character built and unbuilt on a page. The distance between a reader and a character collapsed in implication. The correspondence of the life to the art. The distance dialectical. Material. We feel another's life. Experience individualized in act in a moral interest in a supreme narrative is experience generalized. Two murders. And we want Raskolnikov to escape. We are implicated in the act. The art felt in the life. Supreme narrative a grand constraint of moral interest pursuing consequence on the page in questioning. The consequence of the life. The true real of irrevocable consequence to a character on a page overcome in action caught in moral question. One must act and be judged. One must feel think do live and be judged. There are wise feelings and apt choices. A moral interest come out of the mortal. We want and feel and live and do. Good or bad. Good and bad. All are judged. It is not just. It is necessity. Of self. It is dramatic. It is story. Character. A character come as a consequence. A complication. An implication. The complication moral question in its necessity and ambivalence. Its superimposition of interests and ambivalences infinite in proportion to form. The form never ambivalent. That in the supreme art. The moral proportion of an art in relation to its dramatic interest. An interest in that. There is all aesthetic interest in it. The moral interest of a narrative making an aestheticized interest. Language. Making a complicating language. A moral interest aestheticizing a language in a necessary mortal weight. All the good ever at stake. We want the good for ourselves and another. Yet the question of what should or should not be. How and why to act. That actuality in the art. That the complication. The implication. The complication of one's want. Of the good. We speak of it in a particular way all what we want. The pursuit of the good makes a language. The pursuit of a mortal good sets out the possibility for the aesthetic prosody of a self in moral constraint. For the character of the individual in an art.

For the dramatic picture. It is formal. It is normative. Supreme narrative the moral real pursued in the dramatic confines of the mortal. The want of the good of the individual held hard against the constraint of the historical. The actual. The phenomenal. We want experience. We want experience of the good. There is history. There is the world. In a supreme art the historical cultural political become the phenomenal constraint of the individual character. Of good self. There is the world. The overcoming actuality of experience. All is at stake. We want the good. We act. We are judged. The picture is composed and clear. The good is ever in question. In doubt. In flux. In an ambivalence never to be attenuated. Necessarily it cannot be. The dramatic good in the questioning. In the good of pursuing. One must act in the face of consequence. There is a moral distance to the dramatic. One closes upon it in consequence and questioning. The mortal act the residue of the moral. We want the good for ourselves and another. The pursuit of a good the interest of a life. It is a dramatic questing.

WORKS CITED

Adorno, Theodore. *Negative Dialectics*. Continuum, 1973.

Aristotle. *De Anima (On The Soul)*. Penguin, 1986.

Dostoevsky, Fyodor. *Crime and Punishment*. Knopf, 1992.

Freud, Sigmund. *Civilization and Its Discontents*. W.W.
    Norton & Co., 1961.

Hemingway, Earnest. *A Moveable Feast*. Touchstone, 1996;
    The Sun Also Rises. Scribners. 1926.

James, Henry. *The Art of Fiction*. Printed in: *Essentials of
    the Theory of Fiction*. Duke, 1996.

Joyce, James. *Finnegans Wake*. Penguin, 1976.

Milton, John. *Paradise Lost*. W.W. Norton & Co., 1975.

Plato. *Republic, VII*. Hackett, 1992.

Proust, Marcel. *In Search Of Lost Time*. Modern Library,
    1992.

Schulz, Bruno. *The Street Of Crocodiles*. Penguin, 1977.

Stein, Gertrude. *The Making of Americans*. Dalkey, 1995;
    The Autobiography of Alice B. Toklas. Vintage,
    1960.

www.ingramcontent.com/pod-product-compliance
Lightning Source LLC
LaVergne TN
LVHW011236080426
835509LV00005B/529